The Last and Greatest Revival

APOSTLE DR. MANDLENKHOSI SIMELANE

Revival Life Publishing

Throughout this book, Scripture has been quoted from various Bible translations to bring clarity and depth to the message God has entrusted to us. Unless otherwise noted, the **Amplified Bible (AMP)** has been the primary translation used.

- The **King James Version (KJV)** is in the public domain and may be freely used without permission.

- The **New Living Translation (NLT)** is © 1996, 2004, 2015 by Tyndale House Foundation. Permission has been graciously granted for its use in this publication.

- The **New International Version (NIV)** is © 1973, 1978, 1984, 2011 by Biblica, Inc.® Used by permission. All rights reserved worldwide.

- The **Amplified Bible (AMP)** is © 1954, 1958, 1987, 2015 by The Lockman Foundation. Used by permission. This version has been used predominantly throughout the text.

- The **Amplified Bible, Classic Edition (AMPC)** is © 1954 by The Lockman Foundation. Used by permission.

- The **American Standard Version (ASV)** is in the public domain and may be used freely.

- The **New American Standard Bible (NASB)** is © 1960, 1962, 1963, 1968, 1971, 1972, 1973, 1975, 1977, 1995 by The Lockman Foundation. Used by permission.

- The **New King James Version (NKJV)** is © 1982 by Thomas Nelson, Inc. Used by permission. All rights reserved.

This book is protected by international copyright law, including the provisions of the **Berne Convention** and the **Uniform Commercial Code (UCC)**.

This publication has been assigned the following ISBNs:

Print Edition: 978-0-7978-0770-9
eBook Edition: 978-0-7978-0771-6

No part of this work may be reproduced in any form without prior written consent from the author or publisher, except as permitted by U.S. copyright law.

Author: Apostle Dr. Mandlenkhosi Simelane
Copyright © 2025 by Apostle Dr. Mandlenkhosi Simelane. All rights reserved.

Contents

Introduction: Seliyana	1
1. God Among His People	7
2. The Characteristics of the Greatest Revival	16
3. The Holy Spirit: The Man of the Hour	31
4. A Call to Continuous Repentance	39
5. My Sheep Hear My Voice	48
6. Great Power Comes with Great Responsibility	57
7. Phongola: A Foretaste of Revival	66
8. Prayer is the Engine for Revival	71
9. Dying to Self	84
10. It's Building Time in the Kingdom of God	92
11. The Formation of Christ	106
12. Confrontation Between Right and Wrong	116
13. A Continent Can Be Saved in One Day	128

14. Good Morning Africa	134
15. Every Word of God Will Come to Fulfilment	139
16. Season of the Supernatural	145
17. I Have Come to Cast Fire	158
18. Are You Willing to Pay the Price?	164
19. Young Men of the Provinces	173
20. The Glorious Return	186
Salvation Decision	190
About the author	192
Connect with us	194
Endnotes	196

Introduction: Seliyana

In September 1983, I was filled with the Holy Spirit which marked the beginning of my deeper conversations with God. He told me many great and awesome things He was going to do on earth, to me, and even through me.

At first, I was overwhelmed with excitement at these, His promises, but then He said something that forever changed the course of my life: *"First, you must die to your own will."*

That moment was a turning point of my life, revealing that surrender is the price of being used by God. It wasn't easy to hear, but it was necessary. God was not asking for my talents or my abilities; He was asking for my will. This is what awaits all of us in this great revival.

This is obviously not the first revival to come to planet earth. God once said something that left me surprised: *"There have only been two major revivals in the history of the world: the revival of the Spirit and the revival of the Word."*

He explained that the revival of the Word left the Spirit behind, and the revival of the Spirit left the Word behind. Because of this imbalance, they burned through like a veld fire—intensely burning as they moved forward but dying behind them. It was not a sustainable fire.

But then God said, "*In these last days, I will bring a great revival.*" Notice, He did not call it the third revival; He called it the *last revival*. And He said this revival will be the *greatest revival*.

It will unite both the Word and the Spirit, burning with a fire that will not die out but will grow stronger until it culminates in the return of our Lord Jesus Christ.

For those who do not know what revival looks like, let us look at the traits of two previous mighty revivals: The Welsh Revival and the Azusa Street Revival. Both transformed individuals, families, and even nations.

The Welsh Revival, led by Evan Roberts in 1904, was a powerful move of God that swept through Wales with such intensity that it even made headlines in secular media.[1]

Figure 1: Revival Edition

The Evening Express newspaper famously dedicated a "revival edition" to document the transformative power of this move. Communities were radically changed, pubs closed down due to lack of customers, and crime rates plummeted as multitudes flocked to prayer meetings instead of worldly pursuits.

> # THE WELSH REVIVAL.
>
> ## TWENTY THOUSAND CONVERTS IN SOUTH WALES.
>
> Our Cardiff correspondent wires:—The "South Wales Daily News" returns of converts during the revival, vouched for in every case by the minister or secretary of the churches supplying the returns, give a total of over 20,000 for Glamorganshire, part of Monmouthshire, and part of Breconshire, and this number is being added to daily. Some remarkable results are reported from districts which the revivalists have not yet visited. Thus at Penarth, the Rev.

Figure 2: Reports of widespread salvations

In fact, the Welsh revival was marked by a large number of people getting saved. In a report by the Guardian, a London based newspaper in 1905, over 20,000 people were getting saved in a single district.[2] A high number compared to the population of Wales at the time—around 100,000.

Figure 3: Early Coverage of Azusa Street Revival

The Azusa Street Revival, which began in Los Angeles in 1906, under the leadership of William J. Seymour, birthed the modern Pentecostal movement. Marked by the tangible presence of the Holy Spirit, miracles, and unity across racial and social divides, it demonstrated the power of God to bring people together and transform lives. Secular newspapers like the Los Angeles Times even covered the outbreak of tongues on their front pages.[3]

These two revivals, raging in two parts of the world, were great experiences. But mark this—the revival that is upon us will by far surpass anything we have ever witnessed before. This is the last and greatest revival. It will stretch across every continent, unleashing miracles, signs, and wonders on a global scale. It will usher in the greatest harvest of souls that the world has ever seen and culminate in the return of our Lord Jesus Christ.

The Revival We Need

The revival that God has promised will not come through extraordinary people; it will come through those who are willing—those who have fully surrendered to His will. God is looking for vessels who have died to self, vessels who are ready to carry His glory. This move of God will not be confined to churches or denominations; it will sweep through homes, cities, and entire nations. Young people, in particular, will rise as a powerful force, ignited by the fire of the Holy Spirit to take the gospel to places their religious elders never imagined. But these young people will not be at their own beck and call, they will rely on the wisdom of their elders. Another group that has received a promise are families, they will also be another vehicle for advancing the revival.

Revival doesn't come without preparation. God is calling us to be hungry, prayerful, and surrendered. Revival does not come to those who are complacent—it comes to those who are desperate for more of Him. This book is more than a collection of teachings; it is a call to action. Over the last several decades, God has revealed glimpses of what is coming and how we must prepare. He has shown that prayer and obedience will be the foundation of this move. Without these, we cannot sustain what God desires to accomplish.

The time of revival is not a time to spectate; it is a time to participate. God has chosen this generation—our generation—to carry His glory into the earth. It is no coincidence that you are alive at this moment. The plans of the enemy to destroy you, to derail your destiny, have utterly failed. You were chosen for this time.

As you read this book, my prayer is that it stirs up a holy fire in you—an insatiable hunger to know God more deeply and to position yourself for the role He has assigned you. I do not know where you are in your Christian journey. Perhaps you have not yet made the decision to follow Christ. If that is the case, you will find a salvation prayer at the end of the last chapter. The moment you pray it, you will be saved, and you will join the Kingdom family of God.

If you are already saved, whether you are a mature believer or still new in the faith, I want to encourage you: do not feel intimidated. Do not be overwhelmed by the stories we will share from the Bible, people's experiences, or the testimonies of saints from the past. These stories are not here to discourage you but to stir up hunger in your heart—a longing for more of God.

That is my deepest desire for you as you read this book. Know this: you were saved for such a time as this—the last and greatest move of God. This means that He has seen something in you, and has chosen you to be part of His divine plan. It is now up to you to choose Him back. Take courage in that truth and allow it to fuel your pursuit of Him.

The glorious trumpet has sounded, and already, we can feel the first raindrops of this great revival. But let me tell you—what we've been promised is a downpour, and it's coming. Are you ready for it? In my native Siswati, we have a song we sing: *Seliyana*. It's a prophetic declaration that the rain is here.

The greatest revival in history is here. It is time to take your position, and pay the price to be part of what God is doing in these last days. This is not just a revival—it is the beginning of the end. The Lord Jesus is coming soon! The only question is: Will He find you ready?

Chapter One

God Among His People

"Oh, that You would rend the heavens! That You would come down! That the mountains might shake at Your presence"
   Isaiah 64:1 (NKJV)

When God first spoke to me about revival, I had never heard about the word before. But a few years later, I stumbled upon a pamphlet describing the Welsh Revival, where God mightily used Evan Roberts and others. That is when I realized how powerfully God can shake a nation. As remarkable as that revival and others like it were, they pale in comparison to what God has in store for this greatest and last revival.

It was in the 1980s, just after I had been filled with the Holy Spirit, that the Lord began revealing details of this great revival and the people He would use. Most of these revelations occurred during prayer meetings in my home. In those days, anyone was welcome to join these meetings, regardless of their church or background.

One particular gathering from when I was still working stands out. I had just returned from weekend services led by a pastor from my childhood church. In my early days, I had told that pastor I wanted to accompany him whenever he preached, even if it meant using my leave days on weekdays. I really enjoyed praying for him while he ministered.

After these particular services in Mbabane, Eswatini ended, I returned to my home in Matsapha, Eswatini and found two young men waiting for me. My wife and I ended up in an unplanned prayer session with the two young men visiting our house. We initially engaged in a conversation with them. The next thing we knew it was nearly time for the late last bus they could take home.

"Let's have a quick prayer so you don't miss the bus," I said.

What began as a simple prayer to ensure they caught their bus turned into an all-night encounter with God. We prayed through the night, only stopping at dawn when it was time to leave for work on Monday morning. Though unplanned, the presence of God was undeniable. He spoke extensively—about nations, about individuals—and imparted spiritual "files" into my heart. Many of the insights and revelations I share in this book stem from that extraordinary night of prayer and other similar gatherings that were fueled by our decision to pray for the things that God said on that night.

Among the many things He revealed to me, the most profound was the herald of a coming revival. This revival will not only be the greatest in the history of the earth but also the grand finale—its conclusion will be marked by the return of our Master, Jesus Christ.

As the grand finale, this revival will not only be larger in scale, but it will be operationally distinct. Unlike past revivals that erupted suddenly and ran their course, this one is different. It is unique because God has been preparing the Body of Christ for this moment. Many of God's prophets have spoken about this revival, and churches attuned to the times have focused their efforts on its arrival. It is the desire of God that we are not caught unprepared like the foolish virgins in the parable of the ten virgins (Matthew 25: 1-13).

In preparation for this revival, God is pouring out revelation to shape His Body into the likeness of Christ, raising up the like-sons of God. During this season, we will fully understand why the Bible declares that nature groans in anticipation of the revelation of the sons of God (Romans 8:19). Their unveiling will be a supernatural phenomenon. This book offers not only the opportunity to ignite our excitement but also to prepare us for the imminent revival.

The Onset of the Downpour

Throughout this book, we will often refer to the "coming revival." While it may sound like a contradiction, I do want you to know that the revival is already here. When we talk about the "coming revival" in this context, we are speaking about the full explosion—the grand outpouring.

As we will cover below, we are living in the raindrops of this revival. It has already begun; the initial signs are here. What we are waiting for is the full manifestation—the complete unfolding of God's glorious plan. So, as you read, take heart and know: the revival is not a distant event—it is already underway.

When God first spoke to me about the coming revival, I stood and prophesied. For those keeping track, it has been 40 years of faithfully proclaiming it. The good news is that the divine clock now signals the day of fulfillment. It is no longer a season of prophecy but a season of declaration. We are in the early raindrops of an outpouring that will soon flood the earth.

Those who have watched rain arrive on a clear afternoon know the pattern: One moment, a cloud forms; the next, scattered droplets fall, followed by a steady, heavy rain. In the same way, the revival raindrops we see now are a sign of the greater outpouring that is near. This season, marked by these first drops, confirms that revival is no longer just a prophetic expectation—it is a present reality. God has likened this move to a mighty rain, and the early stirrings we witness across the world are only the beginning. When we speak of "revival", we are not loosely referring to the contemporary term which is often used to describe organized Christian meetings. The revival we are talking about goes far beyond human arrangements—it is about God rending the heavens and coming down to dwell among His people.

This is beautifully captured by the quoted verse at the beginning of the chapter by Prophet Isaiah: "Oh, that You would rend the heavens and come down" (Isaiah 64:1). What we are stepping into now is the fulfillment of this cry. In this day and age, we will witness God moving among His people in an extraordinary way. When God comes, it is unlike you visiting your friend. The glory of His presence carries a weight that transforms everything. In His presence, certain things simply cannot remain—they must give way to His holiness and power.

Conditions For Revival

The aim of this book is to steer people towards the active preparation of this revival. In past revivals, maybe a few people picked up that something was in the air. However, this time we have been given ample time to prepare. That preparation begins with prayer—the incubator of revival. Prayer births revival, thus creating a platform for God to move and fulfill His will.

In these moments of prayer, God speaks directly to His people and stirs their hearts to fall deeply in love with His Word. Igniting a powerful cycle: as people draw closer to God, their hunger for His Word intensifies. This hunger drives a deeper pursuit of Him, fueling an even greater desire to know Him intimately.

In school, most students learn about the necessary conditions for a seed to germinate. Similarly, prayer and repentance are some of the conditions required for revival to germinate. When God's people shift radically from where they are and turn back to Him, they set the stage for His outpouring. Revival doesn't just happen—it responds to hearts actively seeking Him.

You might be asking, how do we even reach the point where revival becomes necessary? Why can't we always be in revival? It happens when two vital things are lost: prayer and a hunger for the Word of God. When God's Word disappears from the corporate Body of Christ, everything tied to Him is lost as well. Without the Word, even the morality of His people is lost. The Psalmist declares;

> **"Your word is a lamp to my feet and a light to my path."** *Psalm 119: 105 (AMPC)*

The power of the Word to cleanse and lead our hearts fades when we lose our hunger for it. Even the Lord Jesus emphasized this truth, calling the Word, heaven's cleansing agent:

> **"Now ye are clean through the word which I have spoken unto you."** *John 15:3 (KJV)*

Many years ago, I heard a story about a man and his son. When the time came for the son to leave home for boarding school, the father gave him a single parting gift—a Bible. Inside, he wrote these words: *"This Book will keep you from sin, but sin will keep you away from this Book."* Simple, yet powerful!

This note captured the power of God's Word: it keeps us pure and guards us against sin. When we lose the Word, we lose our moral compass, leading to the brokenness and moral bankruptcy we see in the world today. But when the Word returns, it brings cleansing and restoration. In the time of revival, God will only work through those who are sanctified by His Word. When this mighty revival breaks out, God will use ready vessels.

The Finishing Generation: Our Role in Revival

You may wonder why God would reserve the greatest revival for what many call the most wicked generation. Looking back at the heroes of faith, it is clear that God was never short of options . Some of these heroes even foresaw this time, but they were told it was not for their day. But here's something that may surprise you: while the focus has always been on us believing in God, today I want you to know that God believes in you.

You may have read in the Bible about John, the beloved disciple, resting on the bosom of the Lord, and perhaps you might even feel a bit envious of that intimacy. But let me tell you, at that time, John did not have the Lord Jesus living inside him. While we may not rest on His bosom, we carry this same Lord within us. The God who comes down is not just with us—He is in us.

I remember one time while preaching in Sri Lanka, God spoke to me clearly: ***"I do not want you to carry big messages to the nations. I want you to carry Me."***

That truth changed everything for me. In this time, we are not just sharing sermons or ideas; we are carrying God Himself. We are carriers of the living God, and that is how greatly you have been chosen by Him. It is an honor He did not reserve for others before us, but for you and me.

I always make an example using a coach assembling a relay team. The best runners are placed as the starter and the finisher, while the middle legs go to the third and fourth best. Here's the good news—our Coach, the Holy Trinity, has chosen us to run the final leg of this race.

It was not for a shortage of people, but it was as though God was handpicking arrows from His quiver, releasing them at appointed times—Noah, Moses, Daniel, the Apostle Paul, the Apostle Peter—and holding you back for a moment like this. It was as though He was saying, "Not this one, I am reserving him for the final stretch." And that final leg is upon us now. But we must seize this moment with humility, not pride.

It's no accident that God has called us to be the finishing generation. He trusts us to carry this revival all the way to the return of His Son, Jesus Christ. But with this great privilege comes great responsibility. As we embrace revival, we must turn away from our old ways, repent of our sins, and focus entirely on our Lord Jesus Christ. This is how we prepare to fulfill our calling and carry this revival to the ends of the earth.

To be effective in this end-time revival, part of our preparation is to be equipped with the ability to hear God's voice. God has made it clear that this revival will be sparked by obedience. But to obey, we must first hear the instruction. When we hear Him, we must obey. The small droplets we see today are a promising sign, but God has promised us a massive outpouring. The arrival of this great outpouring depends on the obedience of a single individual among the over 8 billion people on earth today. We do not know who it will be, but we know that person will obey.

As we journey through this book, we will highlight everything you need to understand and prepare yourself to be part of this end-time move of God. This comes from over 30 years of God speaking and preparing us for revival. It doesn't matter what group, church, race or nationality you identify with—we all have a role to play if we prepare ourselves. While this revival may start with a member of a specific church or nationality, it will not belong to any. Rather, solely to God, spreading across the globe: from nation to nation, from shore to shore, from coast to coast!

Promises of Revival

As this revival sweeps across the globe, it will not just bring spiritual transformation—it will bring social, political, and economic changes as well. For example, in the early days when God was telling me about revival, He told me to look up. While looking up, I saw a dark place shrouded in darkness and covered in soot. Then, a mighty wind blew through the continent, sweeping away the soot. Then God said, *"The place I have shown you is Africa and the wind is revival."*

Through this vision, God revealed that as revival moves through Africa, many of the current challenges will change, and with it, we will see economic development flourish across the continent. People will once again look to Africa as a place with solutions, not just one that is broken and dejected.

This has already started. In 1997, during a tent campaign in Malindza, Eswatini, I had an open vision. I saw a massive Boeing 747 descending to land in the country. The confusing thing was that the only airport we had was far too small to accommodate a plane of that size. It got even more confusing when God indicated the airport would be built in a place called Sikhuphe; it did not make economic sense. The existing airport was within a 30-minute radius of the country's two largest cities, Mbabane and Manzini, while this place in Malindza was over an hour away from Manzini.

God does not lie! What He speaks will always come to pass. Despite opposition, the airport was constructed, two decades later. In hindsight, I am realising that the airport will serve as an entry point for people when they come for the revival in Eswatini. All the economic development we are seeing is part of God's greater plan for revival. Similar to countries preparing for a World Cup, there is a lot of work that has to happen in multiple places to facilitate the great move of people that will happen during this revival. God is aligning the world for the transformation that is coming.

I am reminded of a moment during the preparations for the 2010 World Cup in South Africa—the first in Africa. There were many doubts and concerns about whether the country had capacity to host. Journalists, skeptical and anxious, questioned the then FIFA president whether there was a contingency plan— a "Plan B." His response was unwavering, and with his Swiss accent, he declared, "Plan A is South Africa, Plan B is South Africa, and Plan C is South Africa." In the same vein, I want to tell you this: God's Plan A is revival, Plan B is revival, and Plan C is revival. Heaven has no backup plan because God's Word does not need one. His Word will not fail, and His promises will not tarry.

No matter how bleak things may seem to be in the world today, let me remind you of this unshakable truth: God will fulfill His Word, and the devil has already failed dismally. The chaos, the uncertainty, and the resistance we see around us cannot and will not derail the plan of God. Revival is not just a possibility; it is a certainty. God has spoken, and what He has spoken will come to pass.

A significant portion of this book will focus on God's revelations about the coming revival. These revelations have come through various mediums—dreams, visions, and audible utterances. All of this is part of God's divine plan to prepare us for the great revival that is on the horizon. God has chosen to reveal these truths so that we are not caught unprepared when this mighty revival explodes.

It is my prayer that as you read this book, you will gain a deeper understanding of what this revival will be like. May it stir within you a hunger to be part of this end-time move of God. More importantly, this book will guide you in understanding how you can prepare yourself to be used by God in this revival.

Chapter Two

The Characteristics of the Greatest Revival

"If my people, which are called by my name, shall humble themselves, and pray, and seek my face, and turn from their wicked ways; then will I hear from heaven, and will forgive their sin, and will heal their land."
2 Chronicles 7: 14 (KJV)

Every revival throughout history has had unique characteristics—whether it was the deep revelation of the Word, the use of hymns, or the operations of the Holy Spirit. The Welsh Revival, for instance, was defined by the depth of revelation (the Word), and worship (hymns). In contrast, the Azusa Street Revival, which birthed the modern day Pentecostal movement, was distinguished by a profound and powerful move of the Holy Spirit.

Likewise, God has revealed distinct qualities of the revival to help us prepare and serve as guideposts. Ten key characteristics of this revival are introduced below. In the chapters that follow, we will explore each of them in greater depth.

A Revival of Repentance

The first key marker of this revival will be widespread repentance. Revival hinges on repentance and a return to God and His ways. The headline verse from the book of Chronicles emphasizes the need for individuals to turn away from their self-centered paths and engage in ceaseless prayer. This scripture teaches us that repentance and prayer are necessary to spark the move of God. People from all walks of life will repent without anyone accusing them. We will see public repentance from religious, economic, and political leaders.

God gave us a glimpse of what this looks like during some of our outreach crusades—when His glory fell, people felt naked and exposed in their sinfulness, which led them to repent. This is the same feeling that led Peter to say: **"Go away from me, Lord; I am a sinful man!"** *(Luke 5: 8).*

During one crusade in the Southern part of Eswatini, in a town called Lavumisa, we saw people repenting of things they had done in secret, not just public errors. One man went as far as confessing the theft of his colleague's chewing gum. We often focus on sins like adultery when we think about repentance, but when God's Glory descends, even what we call minor sins feel heavy for our conscience. Yet this exposure is not about condemnation. It is an invitation to return to the Father.

This repentance will turn both Christians and non-Christians toward God. The moment they behold Him, true transformation will take place. Whenever God steps out of heaven and touches the earth, He leaves an indelible imprint. That is why we still talk about the Old Testament revival, when the nation of Israel returned to God after losing their way. The Mount Carmel revival led an entire nation to repentance (I Kings 18: 20 - 39).

A Revival of Ceaseless Prayer

The second characteristic of this revival is that people will pray like never before, triggering a cycle of ceaseless prayer. This beautiful loop of prayer will fuel even more prayer, like a wheel rolling down a hill. As the prayer gains momentum, it will generate power—power that will shake the nations and lead to an explosive demonstration of God's presence. But everything hinges on prayer.

Revival cannot happen unless people pray for it, and our greatest advantage is that God answers prayer. When we pray for what He desires, He responds. For this revival, God places prayers in the hearts of His people, and when they remain faithful in praying, He guarantees an answer. Only God initiates the kind of prayer that brings revival to the earth. God responds to prayers aligned with His will, not our selfish desires. That is why the Lord teaches us to pray, **"Let Your will be done"** (Matthew 6:10). When God deposits a prayer in our hearts and we echo it back to Him, He answers. Our role is to pray with expectant hearts, bringing His purposes and promises into reality.

Many have been praying for revival, and indeed, we are starting to see the first droplets. As mentioned, God likens this revival to a torrential downpour, and I believe the drizzle we see today is only the beginning. Our duty in prayer is to not settle or grow complacent at this early stage; God has promised something infinitely mightier than what we see now—a season of great signs and wonders.

Supernatural Manifestations

The third major hallmark of this last revival will be supernatural manifestations. In the season of the supernatural, when God decides to impose himself on human affairs, the supernatural becomes the new natural. In our time, we will witness more supernatural occurrences until they become commonplace. In this revival, miracles will happen even as people think, and many will be creative in nature, showcasing an abundance of divine displays. Before exploring these supernatural happenings, let me echo the advice Mary gave to the disciples of the Lord Jesus: be ready to do whatever He tells you.

> *"Whatsoever He saith unto you, do it.." John 2:5 (KJV)*

Their obedience unlocked access to the supernatural. In this revival, prompt obedience will be key. Despite the great move of God in Samaria, He told Philip to leave the many people and preach to just one person in the desert. Had Philip delayed—even to pray over the command—he would have missed the chariot. I cannot stress enough the importance of obedience, especially in the realm of the supernatural. Even as the Lord Jesus walked on earth, He kept His eyes and ears fixed on the Father.

> *"So Jesus answered them by saying, I assure you, most solemnly I tell you, the Son is able to do nothing of Himself (of His own accord); but He is able to do only what He sees the Father doing, for whatever the Father does is what the Son does in the same way [in His turn]." John 5:19 (AMPC)*

As exciting as supernatural matters can be, I want to add another word of caution. The first key is obedience, and the second is staying rooted in the Word. When these supernatural events unfold, we must remain grounded in Scripture. During His time of fasting and prayer,

Jesus overcame the devil by standing firmly on the Word. Though the experience of being taken to different places was supernatural, He resisted the enemy by wielding what Paul calls the *Sword of the Spirit—the Word of God* (Ephesians 6:17).

The spiritual realm is vast, containing both good and evil. That is why the Bible instructs us to test every event and prophecy against the Word of God. While God can speak what is not in scripture, He cannot speak what is against it. This fundamental truth must guide our discernment as believers.

The first and most reliable way God speaks to us is through His Word—the Holy Scriptures. Every other way He chooses to speak must align with Scripture, reflecting His unchanging nature and revealed truth.

Obedience and being full of the Word serve as the safety kit for the supernatural. In this revival, people will experience supernatural translations, traveling to countries and regions they have never been to. The Holy Spirit will translate them to preach to other nations, often arriving where crowds are already assembled and hungry for the Word of God. After delivering His message, they will be translated again—shielding them from the risk of pride caused by people worshipping them after these supernatural deeds.

These events may seem new, but they mirror what happened to Philip. The Spirit transported him to the Ethiopian eunuch, and after baptizing him, he was immediately taken to Azotus, where he found people already gathered and preached to them.

> **"When they came up out of the water, the Spirit of the Lord [suddenly] took Philip [and carried him] away [to a different place]; and the eunuch no longer saw him, but he went on his way rejoicing. But Philip found himself at Azotus, and as he passed**

> **through he preached the good news [of salvation] to all the cities, until he came to Caesarea [Maritima]."**
> *Acts 8:39-40 (AMP)*

A Global Revival

The fourth defining characteristic of this revival is its global scale. Although it will break out in Africa, it will not be an African revival but a global move of God. No one will claim ownership as God will orchestrate something beyond human control. It will not be governed by any individual, nation or church—it will be entirely the work of God.

When miracles abound, no one can claim credit. During a mighty move of God in the early days at Madlangemphisi, Eswatini, even children performed miracles. How could any Pastor take credit for that? Unlike past revivals where certain figures rose to prominence and became "superstars," this time it will be different. God is raising many ordinary people across every continent to carry His presence and power. Each of us has a role in bringing His glory to the nations.

I pray that God delivers us from *spiritual nationalism.* We must not fall into the same mindset as the early apostles, who at times tried to see the ministry to the Gentiles through the Jewish lens and limitations (i.e. the issue of circumcision.). Let us embrace His global vision, praying for every nation as fervently as we would for our own.

The Glory of God

The fifth characteristic of this end-time revival is the tangible weight of God's presence descending upon the earth. As His children, we know nothing remains the same when God shows up. Everything changes.

One day, during a crusade in Lavumisa while resting and enjoying sugar cane between services, God spoke to me again and said, **"Smith Wigglesworth only scratched the surface. What you are going to see in this season is going to be an unprecedented level of glory and demonstration of My power."** This revelation left me in awe about the Glory that God was about to release on planet Earth.

When this glory comes, everything will change. The glory of God is not just a light—it is the Lord Jesus Himself. When He descends, strongholds over nations break. Even in my own country, Eswatini, demonic forces will surrender their long-held grip and flee.

I once saw a vision of God moving throughout Eswatini. As I hovered above the country, I witnessed the prayers of believers rising like fiery flames from every corner. From every direction, these prayers surged upwards, connecting as a column that went to heaven. Their fervor ushered in such a mighty manifestation of God's presence that demons could not withstand—they packed their things and left.

Then, miracles began to unfold. Nothing was too difficult; everything became astonishingly easy. We sang songs of praise during that time, and with each note, the impossible became ordinary. The rising of the dead felt as effortless as healing a headache. Even the elderly and those in the highest authorities of this land will be swept into this great move of God, and many of them will walk in prophetic anointing.

I assure you, I have seen a new Eswatini. It is a new and spiritually clean place. The good news is that this experience will not only happen in Eswatini. His glory will sweep across nations, bringing transformation wherever it flows.

Before long, revival will become the talk of the world. Whether through traditional media or as you scroll through social media, testimonies of miracles and undeniable evidence of God's power will capture the attention of nations.

Abundance of Worship

The sixth defining hallmark of this revival is the abundance of worship—a continuous, spontaneous outpouring of praise to the Lord. Worship will be a distinguishing feature in this move of God, with unceasing cries of adoration rising from His people. In this revival, worship will beget miracles, and those miracles will, in turn, spark even greater worship. As God's mighty works unfold, hearts will be overwhelmed with awe, voices will rise in exaltation, and the Lord Himself will inhabit the praises of His people. His presence will usher in more miracles, creating an ever-expanding cycle of worship and divine manifestations.

Consider Paul and Silas in jail (Acts 16:16–34). Though bleeding from their wounds and tightly chained, they sang praises to God at midnight. As they worshiped, the earth shook, prison doors flung open, and chains fell off—yet no prisoner fled. Every prisoner was arrested by the undeniable presence of God. The jailer, overwhelmed and assuming he had lost all the prisoners, prepared to take his own life. Paul stopped him, saying, *"We are all here!"* Convicted and moved by God's power, the jailer fell before them, asking, *"What must I do to be saved?"* No sermon was preached; it was the power of worship that ushered in God's glory and salvation.

Now, take a moment and imagine standing in the midst of worship, witnessing a person without a leg suddenly grow one back and leaping with both legs. Would you need further proof after witnessing such a miracle? People would cry out for salvation instantly. No building, stadium, or auditorium will be able to contain the masses drawn by God's presence. Worship will ignite such a powerful declaration of His glory that people will fall on their knees wherever they are, crying, *"Lord, have mercy!"* This revival will not only transform hearts but also demonstrate God's power in undeniable ways leaving no doubt of His presence among us.

The Revival of the Holy Spirit and the Word

The seventh property of this revival is its defining feature: a perfect union of the Word and the Spirit. Unlike previous revivals that often emphasized one over the other, this last revival will bring both into complete harmony, releasing an unparalleled move of God on the earth. In the past, revivals of the Word were powerful from a doctrinal standpoint, but without the Holy Spirit, they often felt dry and intellectual. Conversely, Spirit-led revivals burned with passion, igniting hearts and spreading quickly like wildfire, yet without the firm foundation of the Word, some lacked depth and a lasting impact.

This time, God is doing something new and unprecedented. He is unleashing both the Word and the Spirit together in perfect balance. The Word will provide a solid foundation, rooting believers deeply in truth and ensuring that the revival is not merely emotional but truly transformative. At the same time, the Spirit will breathe life into that Word, making it active, powerful, and accompanied by signs, wonders, and miracles. This harmony will create a revival that is not only deeply rooted in God's truth but also overflowing with His supernatural power.

The Word and the Spirit are not in competition—they are complementary. The Word brings understanding, while the Spirit brings revelation. The Word teaches us who God is, and the Spirit makes Him real to us. Together, they will ensure that this revival transforms not just minds but hearts, creating a lasting impact on individuals, communities, and nations. The revival of both the Word and the Spirit will bring about a fullness that the Church has never experienced before. It will be like the early Church in the Book of Acts, where doctrine and power worked hand in hand to advance the Kingdom of God.

Unprecedented Faith

The eighth property of this end-time revival is that God is going to unleash a new dimension of faith, coupled with extraordinary creative miracles. Many of the miracles that we will witness in this season will be creative in nature—reminiscent of the profound works seen in Genesis Chapter 1.

In July 2000, God spoke something unforgettable to me: He said He would perform creative miracles that would cause people to believe Genesis 1. To many, the account of God creating the heavens and the earth has remained mere history—a story learned in Sunday school but not deeply believed. However, when people witness the creative miracles firsthand, they will know without a shadow of doubt that the God who created the universe in the beginning is alive and actively moving today.

The Bible tells us that God completed creation in six days, but His number of completion is seven. That means there remains one day of creation—a season where God will move in extraordinary ways. When the Bible says that with God, a day is like a thousand years and a thousand years like a day (II Peter 3:8), it reminds us that we are not talking about a 24-hour day but seasons of divine activity. In this final season of creation, The Lord Jesus will not act alone; He will work with His Bride, the Church.

Together with the Lord Jesus, the Church will usher in extraordinary creative miracles across the earth. I am not talking about the common healings that excite us today. Limbs will grow where there were none, eyes will form in empty sockets, and organs will appear where there was once nothing. I do not know about you, but I long to witness these creative acts of God. I have seen glimpses—angels bringing lungs from heaven to people with respiratory failure and replacing failing hearts—but now I yearn to see even more: legs growing, arms forming, and unprecedented displays of God's creative power. This is not an afterthought. God predestined this from the beginning and designed it for His glory.

His plan for this time is truly extraordinary. To give you a sense of how remarkable this revival will be, let me share a personal story. One day, I cried out to God, lamenting that our nation had not experienced revival while others had seen a full experience.

"*Shut up!*"

That was God's startling response. I fell silent, not out of obedience to the command, but because of the shock that gripped me. It was the first time I heard Him speak like that to me.

Then He said,

"*What I have prepared for this season will make it seem as though Moses was playing Sunday school.*"

The full weight of this statement did not hit me until years later. I was reading scripture in Corinthians that declares what Moses experienced does not compare to the coming glory:

> **"For if the ministry of condemnation had glory, the ministry of righteousness exceeds much more in glory. For even what was made glorious had no glory in this respect, because of the glory that excels."** 2 Corinthians 3:9-10 (NKJV)

That is when it dawned on me—what is coming is beyond anything we have ever imagined. Think of all that Moses witnessed in the desert—the burning bush, the plagues in Egypt, the parting of the Red Sea, and the provision in the wilderness. Yet, this dispensation could not be called glory when compared to our time. God Himself likens it to mere child's play in comparison to what is to come. What lies ahead will far surpass it, in ways we can scarcely grasp. It will be a time of overwhelming miracles, signs, wonders, and the glory of God descending upon the earth in an unprecedented way.

To carry out these creative miracles, God will release a new kind of faith—not merely faith in God, but the faith of God. This will be a faith so powerful and unshakable that it aligns us directly to His divine will. During one of our conferences, God revealed that this faith would shine brightly in this season, enabling His people to achieve the impossible. It is paramount for us to ask the Lord for this God kind of faith, which transcends natural understanding and empowers us to operate in His supernatural realm.

Mass Exodus from False Religions

The ninth hallmark will be the mass exodus of people from false religions. This final harvest will be a bumper one, unlike anything we have ever seen. What is coming will remarkably amaze the world. We are at the brink of the greatest exodus in history as multitudes will leave false religions, their eyes finally opened to see the Lamb of God. This isn't just a movement of people but a supernatural awakening where many will encounter the Lord Jesus in extraordinary ways that go beyond preaching—He will simply appear to them.

The conviction that will follow will be so overwhelming that they will run, desperately seeking someone to guide them to salvation. It will not be about human effort but the undeniable move of the Spirit of God, breaking every barrier of unbelief. Even those whose hearts have been hardened for years will find their resistance melting in the presence of God's glory.

In fact, the Lord Jesus has already begun showing Himself to people from various religions, including in regions where preaching the gospel has been restricted—places like Islamic States. The Lord is now appearing directly to individuals, bypassing closed doors and man-made limitations, demonstrating that He is Lord over all. This property of revival signifies that no stronghold is too great and no place is too dark for the light of Christ to reach. This will be the final and greatest harvest—a testament to the relentless love and power of our God.

A Revival Without End

The tenth, and perhaps most thrilling, characteristic of this end-time revival is its eternal nature—it will not die down. Unlike previous revivals that burned brightly for a season but eventually fizzled out, this revival will continue to progressively increase and intensify. It will move wave by wave, glory to glory, and strength to strength, becoming a divine crescendo that ushers in the return of our Lord Jesus Christ. While past revivals often resembled veld fires—blazing fiercely but temporary—this revival will be unquenchable, gaining unstoppable momentum with each passing moment.

The revival will not be a mere historical moment to be remembered but a living, active move of God that transforms the present and future. It will cross every barrier—cultural, geographical, and denominational uniting the Body of Christ like never before.

As it sweeps across nations and continents, the revival will fulfill the ancient prophecies. **"The glory of the Lord will cover the earth as the waters cover the sea"** (Habakkuk 2:14). The knowledge of God's glory will saturate every corner of the earth—For His Word is sure.

At its peak, when the earth resounds with worship, the testimony of the Gospel, and the manifestation of God's glory, the trumpet will sound. God revealed a powerful vision to me about this, which I will share in the final chapter of this book. But one truth is undeniable, JESUS IS COMING BACK. The revival will not end but will signal the culmination of all history—the glorious return of Jesus Christ.

The revival will not fade into history but will culminate in the most awaited event of eternity: the wedding of Christ and His bride, the Church.

Recap: The Characteristics of the Coming Revival

Revival has always carried unique markers, tailored by God to its time and purpose. The coming revival is no exception—it will be the greatest move of God the world has ever seen, defined by ten distinct properties that demand our attention and preparation.

1. **A Revival of Repentance:** The hallmark of this revival will be widespread repentance, as God's glory descends and exposes sin—not for condemnation, but as an invitation to return to Him.

2. **A Revival of Ceaseless Prayer:** Prayer will be the engine driving this move of God, igniting a self-sustaining cycle of intercession and unleashing God's power to shake nations and manifest His glory.

3. **Supernatural Manifestations:** This revival will feature extraordinary supernatural acts, including creative miracles, healings, and supernatural translations.

4. **A Global Revival:** Though it will begin in Africa, this revival will not be confined to one continent.

5. **The Glory of God:** God's tangible glory will descend upon the earth, transforming lives, communities, and nations.

6. **Abundance of Worship:** Unceasing worship will define this

revival. Miracles will beget praise and praise will beget miracles and this will be a continuous cycle

7. **A Revival of the Spirit and the Word:** The end time revival will be defined by a perfect union of the Word and the Spirit.

8. **Faith for Creative Miracles:** God will release a new level of faith—the faith of God—empowering creative miracles that reveal His power as Creator.

9. **A Mass Exodus:** There will be a mass exodus from false religions, as multitudes encounter the Lord Jesus directly.

10. **A Revival Without End:** Unlike past revivals that faded, this one will not end but will culminate in the return of Jesus Christ.

Each of these characteristics highlights the magnitude and scope of what God is about to do. This revival will demand our full participation—not as spectators, but as surrendered vessels through which God can work mightily.

In the next chapter, we will dive deeper into the Holy Spirit, the Man of the hour in this revival. It is He who orchestrates, empowers, and sustains this mighty move of God. Let us prepare our hearts to know Him more intimately and walk fully in step with Him. The revival is here; the Holy Spirit is ready to move. Are we ready to follow?

Chapter Three

The Holy Spirit: The Man of the Hour

"But I tell you the truth, it is to your advantage that I go away; for if I do not go away, the Helper (Comforter, Advocate, Intercessor—Counselor, Strengthener, Standby) will not come to you; but if I go, I will send Him (the Holy Spirit) to you [to be in close fellowship with you]."
John 16:7 (AMP)

Miracles, translations and all activities will unfold under the guidance of the Holy Spirit. However, sadly a lot of people have limited the Holy Spirit, largely because they do not know that He is a Person.

For many, this is often exacerbated by limitations introduced by linguistic nuances. For example, many Southern African languages equate "Spirit" with "soul" or "wind." Don't let that confuse you: the Holy Spirit isn't just a force—He's the third Person of the Godhead, chosen by God to be our Guide in this season. To borrow an everyday phrase, He is the "Man of the Hour."

To understand the importance of the Holy Spirit, consider how the

Lord Jesus introduced Him. As He prepared to depart from this earth, the Lord told His disciples it was better for Him to go so that the Holy Spirit could come (John 16: 7). As you would know, I was not there. However, I do imagine this came as a shock to the disciples who had seen the Lord heal many and feed thousands from five loaves and two fish. Yet the reason is simple: when the Lord Jesus was physically in Jerusalem, He could not simultaneously be in London, Manzini, New York, or Beijing. The Holy Spirit, however, exists in multiple places at once—presenting an immeasurable advantage for the Church today.

The Person of The Holy Spirit

As powerful as the Spirit is, He is a very sensitive Being. Speaking to the church in Thessalonica, Apostle Paul issues a stern warning:

> *"Do not quench [subdue, or be unresponsive to the working and guidance of] the [Holy] Spirit"* 1 Thessalonians 5:19 (AMP)

There is no revival without the Holy Spirit. He is the very essence of revival, the life-breath of the Church, and the power behind every move of God. However, the presence of the Holy Spirit alone is not enough. His presence carries no weight if we are not going to obey Him. Repeated disobedience quenches Him and renders Him ineffective.

The Lord Jesus understood this more than most and that is what increased the efficiency of His ministry. In the Bible, we come across a story where **"It was necessary for Him to go through Samaria"** (John 4: 4). The reason He had to explain this decision to go through Samaria to the disciples, who were Jewish, is that Jews and Samaritans did not see eye to eye.

There was hostility between Jews and Samaritans dating back to the times of the first exile: Samaritans were the product of intermingling of Jews and Assyrian settlers. The tension escalated further when the Samaritans opposed the Jews efforts to rebuild Jerusalem—deepening the divide between the two groups. Despite this historical context, He obeyed the leading of the Holy Spirit and went through Samaria.

When the Lord Jesus met the Samaritan woman, His obedience bore immediate fruit: an entire city turned back to God, marking a city-wide revival. Without obedience, this would have been impossible. Jesus Christ obeyed despite public opinion—leading to a transformational move of God. This example shows how one person's obedience, even at a personal cost, can trigger a revival.

As we covered earlier, the explosion of this great revival hinges on the obedience of just a single individual. One person, heeding the promptings of the Holy Spirit, will ignite the greatest revival the world has ever known. That is why the theme of obedience will be emphasised in the chapters to follow. That individual could be you and I want you to be ready to obey the leading of the Holy Spirit when the time comes.

Love and Unity

The Holy Spirit is important for our effectiveness in the revival because of the building blocks He brings. The first revival building block He brings to the Church is unity—the same unity displayed by the Trinity. During this remarkable revival, God has placed much emphasis on unity among believers. When the Church reflects the love shared by the Father, Son, and Holy Spirit, our environment becomes fertile ground for revival to flourish—to continue with the agricultural metaphor.

The building block that we will spend more time on in this chapter is: love. Ultimately, love creates the atmosphere for revival to thrive. It brings unity and acceptance. We are used to the saying—"everything blossoms in the atmosphere of love". As long as we follow the Holy Spirit's leading and obeying His promptings, we will experience the full power of God's move.

Love must saturate the Church—becoming an aroma which the world will be drawn to. This is an aroma of genuine care and compassion. For far too long, people have claimed they find more love in the secular world than inside the Church. Yet one of the things that God told us about this revival and this supernatural love is that, *"we will love each other as though we have been bewitched."* That time is coming, and it has already begun. In fact, the prophecy has caught up with me and I truly love God's people. I am living in the fullness of that love.

This love will extend beyond denominational barriers, forging unity across multiple congregations. Such unity matters because God has declared that this revival belongs to the entire body of Christ, not just a single gathering. This is the level of love that can empower brethren to still celebrate God while He uses others outside our "own" churches. It can only come from Him. In the early Church, this same love led believers to sell their homes and land to support those in need. Imagine the impact when today's Church is overwhelmed by that love—it will be life-changing.

Ministers of the Gospel especially must be consumed by this love. God recently visited me and said,

"You have no right to preach to people you do not love."

This profound statement shows us God's standard. Let me emphasize this to any minister reading this, love is the key to serving everyone during this revival.

Removing the obstacles

While love is powerful, certain obstacles can blunt its effectiveness.

Removing these impediments is a crucial step to preparing yourself for this end-time revival. Chief among them is unforgiveness—a cancer to unity. That is why the Lord Jesus taught that if someone is offended, they should not go on praying as though everything is fine. Instead, He instructed us to turn back, resolve the offence, and then proceed in prayer (Matthew 5:23). This charge is directed at both the offended and the offender.

In fact, the Lord consistently emphasized forgiveness. When teaching His disciples how to pray, He told them to ask from the Father the same forgiveness they mete unto others.

> *"And forgive us our sins; for we also forgive every one that is indebted to us. And lead us not into temptation; but deliver us from evil." Luke 11:4 (KJV)*

When impediments like unforgiveness are removed and replaced with the building blocks of love and unity, we will experience the outpouring of the Holy Spirit. I could point to the first Church in Acts, but let's consider a more recent example. William Seymour, a key figure in the Azusa Street Revival, upheld these foundational principles at a great personal cost. Living in a racially segregated America, he faced severe challenges. In Bible school, he was barred from sitting with white students and had to listen to lectures from the hallway or outside. Yet, Seymour's heart of forgiveness positioned him to be used mightily by God for an extraordinary outpouring of the Holy Spirit.

Likewise, we must remove everything that hinders the Holy Spirit's work in this end-time revival. When we do, we will witness another mighty outpouring—one that unleashes supernatural power and authority upon the Body of Christ. This is why Jesus instructed His disciples to tarry in Jerusalem until they received power (Luke 24:49).

That divine power was essential for fulfilling the Great Commission, and when it manifests, undeniable signs and wonders follow. Multitudes will experience miraculous healings and deliverance from long-standing afflictions.

This is the Holy Ghost Power! Tragically, some ministers today, feeling pressured to perform miracles, have sought power from other sources. But there is only one true source—the Holy Spirit. Without Him, there is no power. Without Him, there is no revival.

Power in Revival

Let me share a vision I had years ago to illustrate this power. I moved through various churches, and as I entered each one, the people inside were filled with shame. I didn't stay long before I found myself on the streets—where I saw an overwhelming number of lame people, far more than I had ever seen. One detail that stood out for me was their frail, thin legs.

Then suddenly, the power of the Holy Spirit was released. Their weak legs grew strong, and they stood, lifting their hands in worship. At that moment, I sang a song I am certain will echo in the coming revival: *"He is my God, and I will love Him forever."*

A powerless church is a church in shame—just like in the vision. But when God's power is restored and miracles unfold, that shame will vanish, replaced by worship and awe. This is the purpose of divine power: to ignite worship and draw people closer to Him.

As the world witnesses creative miracles, the undeniable Hand of God will be witnessed. New legs will grow where there were stubs. Perforated hearts will be made whole. The power of God will be so tangible that even young children will demonstrate it.

Amidst these wonders, we will sing: *"If you need the power, you can get the power now. If you need the power, come get the power now."* No longer will the Church be ashamed. No one will ask, *"Where is their God?"* He will be evident to all. This is the power that will accompany the outpouring of the Holy Spirit.

However, power comes with a prerequisite for me and you. The Lord Jesus was led by the Holy Spirit, and so must we as the sons of God. This is the most crucial aspect of our lives: obedience to the Holy Spirit, following His leadership, and submitting to His direction. Without this, we risk missing the fullness of God's plan for us.

Here is a key piece of advice—if you want to succeed in your walk with God, embrace these principles:

1. **Live a holy life.** Holiness is the foundation for fellowship with God. It keeps the lines of communication open and allows the Holy Spirit to dwell within us without hindrance.

2. **Pray.** Prayer is your lifeline, the means you align your heart with His will. It keeps your spirit sensitive to His voice.

3. **Listen to the Holy Spirit.** Attune your heart to His voice and let His guidance override every other influence.

I often tell people to disregard the opinions of the world and obey God without hesitation. Sadly, some people fear the disapproval of men more than they fear God. Even when God speaks clearly, they hesitate, asking, "What will others think?"

Follow these principles consistently. If you stumble, do not dwell on your mistakes; repent and keep moving forward in obedience to Him.

Hunger is Key

You may be reading this and are not yet been filled with the Holy Spirit. I want you to know—He is closer than you think. The Holy Spirit has already been given. Ours is simply to *hunger* for Him and receive Him.

One of the saddest parts of my walk with God is that although I was saved young, I did not receive the Holy Spirit until years later. I remember the day it finally happened. They called for people to come forward to receive the Spirit, but I didn't go.

But while singing a song about God sending fire, I found myself singing it not in Siswati—but in other tongues. Just like that. It exploded. I felt like I was walking the corridors of heaven. At that moment, God opened me up. I began speaking prophetically to people in the tent, telling them what He was saying about and to each one of them. The power of God held me so long that by the time I came to, the service was over. Only my wife had stayed behind to wait for me.

From that moment, He began to share all manner of things with me. He will make your life, ministry, and calling far more effective. Don't let fear or tradition hold you back. The Spirit of God is available—right now. All you have to do is *hunger* and *receive*.

In the chapters that follow, we will explore how God wants us to prepare for this revival. We will learn the importance of repentance and how to cultivate a heart that keeps the presence of the Holy Spirit alive and unquenched. A sensitive and repentant heart is key to walking in step with the Holy Spirit and being a qualified vessel in this time of revival.

Chapter Four

A Call to Continuous Repentance

"So repent (change your mind and purpose); turn around and return [to God], that your sins may be erased (blotted out, wiped clean), that times of refreshing (of recovering from the effects of heat, of reviving with fresh air) may come from the presence of the Lord"
   Acts 3:19 (AMPC)

When Christians hear the word 'repentance', they often associate it solely with sinners. However, such a limited perspective diminishes its true meaning. In this chapter's scripture, Peter calls everyone to repent. The Amplified Bible describes repentance as: "A change of mind and purpose, turning around, and returning to God." This shows that repentance is not just for the unsaved—it is just as essential for believers.

When the Lord does something new on the earth, it is truly new—unlike anything we have seen or experienced before. This is not just a statement—it is a call to action. This call goes beyond turning from sin. To be properly aligned with this new move, we must change our minds. If we fail to do so, our unrepentant mindset will block us from accessing what God is doing in this season. True repentance, as defined by the Amplified Bible, enables us to fully turn towards God and embrace His fresh work in our lives.

> **"See, I am doing a new thing! Now it springs up; do you not perceive it? I am making a way in the wilderness and streams in the wasteland."** Isaiah 43:19 (NIV)

This verse teaches us that God can do something new, yet it is entirely possible to miss it. A lack of repentance—unwillingness to change our mindset, can blind us to His work. Our minds determine what we are able to receive. If we do not realign ourselves with heaven's agenda, we risk operating at a different frequency than God.

The first shall be last

It is possible for the religious to be left behind while sinners advance. For the longest time, people have taken pride in the many years they have been saved, but the scripture reminds us,

> **"So the last shall be first, and the first last.."**
> *Matthew 20:16 (ASV)*

This speaks to the stark reality that those coming to Christ now are often outpacing those who have been in the faith for years. We will see this even in this time of revival. The newly saved will run with so much fresh zeal, embracing what God is doing, while some of us, who have been saved longer, risk becoming complacent. We should never get used to God!

I remember this one time we were at a tent meeting, and a lady came forward to testify. She said when she first arrived, she thought, "I've been to camps, I've been to tents, what new thing could I possibly learn in this revival meeting?"

But as the meetings went on, God opened her heart. Suddenly, she realized:

"Wait, I do not know this. I do not know that."

In that moment, the pride and resistance in her heart crumbled. God began to move mightily in her life, even healing her of long-standing afflictions.

This is what we mean when we say, turn and behold the new thing that God is doing (Isaiah 43:19). Do not hold on so tightly to your past experiences or salvation journey that you miss what God is doing now. He is doing something new, and it requires a fresh perspective and an open heart to embrace it fully.

The same thing happened when the Lord Jesus came on earth, the religious leaders of His time missed what God was doing. Meanwhile, those least expected; the prostitutes and tax collectors, violently pressed into God's Kingdom. The religious sects of the time were left behind. Even worse, their unrepentant hearts led them to reject Him altogether. They denied who He was, and they crucified Him, simply because, in their minds, there was no way He could be the Son of God.

Their spiritual blindness is still difficult to comprehend. In broad daylight, the religious leaders refused to recognize the Son of God.

If the Pharisees did not know, who should have known?
If the Sadducees did not know, who should have known?

Even when sinners were humbling themselves at the feet of Jesus Christ, the Pharisees still stood back in judgment, Luke records:

> *"Now when the Pharisee who had invited Him saw it, he said to himself, If this Man were a prophet, He would surely know who and what sort of woman this is who is touching Him—for she is a notorious sinner (a social outcast, devoted to sin)."* Luke 7:39 (AMPC)

Even as others press violently into the Kingdom, some still refuse to enter. Consider the harlot who came to the Lord Jesus, kneeling, kissing, and washing His feet with her tears. She ignored the disapproving glances and whispers, pressing into His presence without shame or hesitation. That was a violent, determined entry into the Kingdom. Yet, those who were religious stood back and scoffed, saying, "What is th is?"

I tell you now, this should be a cautionary tale for us. Knowledge of Scripture alone does not guarantee alignment with God. If we are not careful, pride can keep us out of what God is doing, just as it did with the Pharisees.

Experiencing God While in an Illegitimate Position

The greatest revival is upon us, and I want you to grasp this truth: The key to accessing what heaven is releasing into the earth is repentance. Repentance means more than turning from sin; it means changing your mindset, challenging your long-held beliefs, and a refusal to rely on yesterday's revelation. Even what God once decreed may no longer be valid in this season. When it's time has passed, they become illegitimate. Clinging to it may place you outside of God's current move.

Many assume that experiencing God confirms that they are in the right place. Some might even say, *"But I still experience God!"* As you read this, understand: it is possible to experience God while standing in an illegitimate position. To ensure there is no misunderstanding, let us explore a couple of stories from the Bible.

The first and perhaps most striking example in Scripture is the story of the children of Israel. If anyone could claim they experienced God, it was them.

- They witnessed miracles daily: manna and meat fell from heaven.

- They saw the pillar of cloud every morning and the pillar of fire every night.

- Their enemies and their walled cities crumbled before them.

By all accounts, they could have said, *"We see God every day—surely, we are in the right place!"*

But here is the sobering truth: Experiencing miracles does not mean you are in alignment with God. The Israelites wandered in the wilderness for 40 years, living in a state of disobedience. Even after God had decreed that they would perish in the wilderness, He continued to miraculously provide for them and withheld His judgement.

Let that sink in. Miracles are not a sign of divine approval. We must seek to stand in the right place before God and not simply marvel at what He does for us.

Acts of grace, though abundant, should not be mistaken as validation of our alignment with God. The only accurate position for us is to stand on *Mount Zion*—the place where God knows us and a place where we are aligned with His will. The sad reality is that some people will only realize on judgment day that they were never truly in alignment with God. Even the Lord Jesus warns us about this tragic possibility. Let us ensure we are not among those.

> *"Many will say to Me on that day, 'Lord, Lord, did we not prophesy in Your name, and in Your name cast out demons, and in Your name perform many miracles?' And then I will declare to them publicly, 'I never knew you; depart from Me, you who practice lawlessness.'"* Matthew 7:22-23 (NASB 1995)

Repentance is not a one-time event; it is an ongoing posture of the heart. I want us to understand that repentance is crucial in moving with God at all times. It does not matter what you experienced yesterday. It does not matter what God did through you in the past. Today is a new day! What matters is whether you are still in alignment with God today. Let us remain humble, pliable, and willing to move when He moves.

Our second example is King Saul. He once experienced God in a remarkable way—the Spirit of God came upon him, and he prophesied among the prophets. Picture this, one moment he was prophesying alongside them, and the next, God was telling Samuel to stop mourning for Saul because He had rejected him.

> **"How long will you mourn for Saul, since I have rejected him as king over Israel?"** *1 Samuel 16:1 (NASB)*

Saul, who had once walked in the power of God, ended his reign in disgrace, clinging to a throne that no longer belonged to him. Instead of repenting, he spent his final days in an illegitimate position, desperately trying to hold onto what had already been taken away from him.

We must seek to experience God in the now and ensure we are standing in an accurate position before Him. Do not glory in the memories of past encounters with God. Do not hold onto what He has already moved away from. Staying in step with God's current move—His "wave of the now"—is the only way to fulfill His will in our time and season.

God is looking for people who are willing to change their minds, realign their inner being with His will and purpose, and walk in repentance. That is what the devil truly fears—not the institution of the church, but a changed people—a people fully aligned with God.

Repentance from Culture

The third example we will examine has a good ending. Apostle Peter—a man who did not hold onto an illegitimate position, but instead embraced the wave of the now.

This verse below reveals the vital truth: God does not respect our cultural boundaries or traditions when they stand in the way of His plans. We must be prepared for the times when God challenges what we have long held as normal. Peter had to repent—he had to change his mind and align with the new thing that God was doing.

> **"And there came a voice to him, saying, Rise up, Peter, kill and eat. But Peter said, No, by no means, Lord; for I have never eaten anything that is common and unhallowed or [ceremonially] unclean. And the voice came to him again a second time, What God has cleansed and pronounced clean, do not you defile and profane by regarding and calling common and unhallowed or unclean."** Acts 10:13-15 (AMPC)

Peter had spent his entire life refraining from anything deemed unclean, in full obedience to Jewish laws and customs. Yet, suddenly, God challenged everything Peter knew and told him to do something that violated his cultural and religious upbringing. This was no small shift—what Peter had always believed to be *unclean* was now being declared clean by God.

We know that after this, Peter was sent to preach to Cornelius, which opened the door(s) of ministry to the Gentiles. Yet this was not easy, even for the Christians in Jerusalem. But even this new move of God was difficult for the early Christians to accept.

The Jewish believers in Jerusalem questioned Peter for preaching to the Gentiles, holding tightly to their traditions (Acts 11:2-3). However, God had given Peter the key to unlock the door of salvation for all the nations. Had Peter refused to repent and embrace God's new direction, the spread of the Gospel to the world would have been delayed.

Change is in the Air

Change is the buzzword—there must be repentance, and there must be change.

Revival demands repentance—not just from sin, but from outdated mindsets. The greatest obstacle to God's move is often our unwillingness to change.

The Pharisees missed the Messiah whilst clinging to tradition. Early believers struggled with Gentile salvation because it challenged their views. Likewise, resisting change can cost us the 'now move of God'. God is calling us to open hearts and renewed minds. Those stuck in the past will miss His power, but those who move with Him will walk in His presence.

The greatest revival is at hand. Will you be ready?

In the next chapter, we will explore one of the most critical aspects of this revival—hearing and obeying God's voice. God is always speaking, but are we listening?

We will discuss the many ways God speaks, the importance of streamlining His voice and how obedience positions us for greater encounters. In this revival, hearing God is not optional—it is essential. Those who hear and obey will be the ones who carry His power and walk in supernatural alignment with His will.

Let us move forward with open ears, surrendered hearts, and ready spirit to embrace everything God is doing. But it all begins with repentance.

Chapter Five

My Sheep Hear My Voice

> *"The sheep that are My own hear My voice and listen to Me; I know them, and they follow Me."*
> **John 10:27 (AMP)**

God's voice alone has shaped history, secured battles, and transformed lives. To truly benefit from it, we must be His sheep. Make it your determined purpose to obey when He speaks. Your response to His voice will either elevate or diminish your life.

Obedience brings breakthrough, whilst disobedience brings loss. King Saul heard God's command but chose to disobey, and it cost him his destiny.

As we discussed earlier, the genesis of this revival will come from someone hearing and acting. Obedience, while critical, is impossible if we are spiritually deaf. God often gives step by step instructions, revealing more as we follow. If we do not train ourselves to hear and obey every word, we risk falling out of alignment with Him.

Recognising the Voice of God

By now, you should understand the importance of obedience—it is the key to effectiveness in this revival. However, obedience is impossible without being able to recognise the voice of God. Every believer must learn to recognize His voice.

This revival is ordained and directed by God. For us to follow Him, we must hear Him clearly. If you do not yet hear Him, invest time in learning how. In my next book I will be sharing insights on *Streamlining the Voice of God*—a book dedicated to helping believers hear God clearly. It will provide biblical guidance and practical steps to helping you develop sensitivity to His voice.

In *Streamlining the Voice of God*, we will explore the various ways God speaks—drawing from Scripture and real-life testimonies that demonstrate His diverse ways of communication. Below is a brief guide to some of the ways God speaks:

- **The Voice of the Conscience** – The still, small voice within that guides us toward righteousness and makes us shun sin.

- **The Word of God** – Scripture is the foundation of all divine communication, including direction, correction, and unchanging truth.

- **Revelation** – God can instantly deposit divine insight into your spirit, unlocking truths that would take months to grasp.

- **The Holy Spirit** – God's active presence within us, speaking truth, revealing His will, and guiding us into all understanding.

- **The Audible Voice** – Though rare, God sometimes speaks in an audible voice, leaving no doubt that He has spoken.

- **The Gifts of the Spirit** – God communicates through prophecy, word of wisdom, and word of knowledge—bringing insight and direction.

- **Dreams** – Many times, God provides insight, warnings, or direction through dreams.

- **Visions** – Like dreams, visions bring spiritual clarity and deeper understanding of God's plans.

Hearing God is not optional in this revival—it is a requirement. He is speaking now, and we must be ready to listen and obey. Having walked with God for over 60 years, I have learned many lessons about hearing His voice. In this chapter, I will share cautionary stories from my journey—insights to help you navigate this revival with all the sensitivity you need for His leading.

We should hear God before He has to resort to using "sign language." God created you with ears, so why wouldn't He speak to you through them? (Proverbs 20:12). When we ignore His voice, He is often forced to communicate through circumstances, signs, and disruptions. It is far better to hear Him clearly the first time than to require drastic measures.

Lessons from Mfekayi

A perfect example of this happened during a mission trip to Mfekayi in KwaZulu-Natal, South Africa. We had gone to preach, and God moved mightily—His presence was tangible and miracles were widespread.

In the presence of God, extraordinary things began to happen. One of our brethren danced for two weeks—almost nonstop—while prophesying the entire time. I assure you: two weeks of continuous prophecy! That's an incredible flow of divine intervention. Her face even began to radiate like the face of an angel.

It was a glorious time, but despite all of this, we failed to fully listen to God.

We had planned to stay for one week, but God had different plans. Instead of asking Him what He desired, we were fixated on our schedule. And so, God had to resort to "sign language".

Let me ask you this question. Are you truly willing to hear God even when His answer disrupts your plans?

At the end of our first week, heavy rains suddenly fell, destroying the roads and making it impossible for us to leave. God forced us to stay. What should have been a joyful obedience became a forced delay. Had we truly heard God, we would have stayed willingly, not reluctantly.

Looking back, I regret that our ears were not tuned enough to hear His voice directly. Because we remained, lives were saved—people who were destined to die lived. But I still wonder: what more could God have done if we had obeyed freely?

This experience taught me invaluable lessons:

- It is critical that our ears remain tuned to God's voice.

- When He speaks, we must hear and respond willingly, not reluctantly.

- God speaks for our benefit, and not our convenience.

All believers must recognise the voice of God, as the safety, success, and prosperity of God's people depends entirely on their ability to hear His voice. This message is not just for preachers but to all who desire to be used by God in this revival. For instance, a notable group are those God wants to raise as kingdom financiers. While some of these people may already have experience in the marketplace, they cannot rely solely on their own understanding. They must hear God, guiding them on how to grow their wealth and gaining fresh, innovative business ideas.

They must hear God for:
- **Divine strategies** on how to grow their wealth.

- **Fresh, innovative business ideas** that come straight from heaven.

- **Opportunities that others cannot see** because they are tuned to God's frequency.

Wherever God has placed you, you must learn to hear Him. Look at Joseph—he thrived in a foreign land, not because of his own wisdom, but because he obeyed God. His ability to hear and obey turned adversity into success. The same will be true for those who align their ears to God's voice in this time of revival. Will you be one of them?

Disobedience is Costly

Let me share another story to emphasize the importance of obedience. One Friday afternoon, back when I was still working, I was preparing to go preach at a certain place. Just as I was about to leave, a thought crossed my mind:

"It's not safe to travel without a jack."

The issue? That thought came from my mind, not my spirit. It is not our minds that should inform our actions; it is our spirit that must lead us. Despite that, I decided to buy a jack. Instantly, an internal struggle began in my spirit. My spirit resisted but my mind kept insisting, "There's no jack in the car." Looking back, why did I not trust that the One who made air could also ensure there was air in my tires?

The battle in my spirit grew so intense that I began to sweat. Still, I persisted. I even asked a fellow brother to accompany me to the auto parts shop. He agreed but refused to drive. No matter how much I insisted, he would not budge. With the turmoil in my spirit still raging, I drove. All the while, I was praying in tongues—but let me tell you, praying in tongues while being disobedient does not help.

The auto parts shop was just a five-minute drive from work. As my companion and I approached a set of traffic lights, they turned green.

Suddenly, he screamed:

"Careful!"

Before I could react, an oncoming car slammed into us. Even as everything unfolded, I kept praying in tongues—but the lesson was already clear. Disobedience is costly.

After getting out of the car, I walked up to the man who hit us and casually asked:

"Do you see how important it is to accept the Lord Jesus? If we had died, where would you have gone?"

When the police arrived, the man explained that he had not slept for two nights because his wife was in the hospital. But in my heart, I knew where the real fault lay—it was with me. I had ignored the Holy Spirit's leading. I had relied on my own reasoning. And disobedience was costly. So, I told the man not to worry about repairs. Yes, he had made a mistake, but I had made a greater mistake—I disobeyed God. I reiterate: disobedience is costly.

This experience taught me a lesson I will never forget: it is crucial to hear God and submit to His leading. We must be sensitive to the gentle nudges of the Holy Spirit.

Tuning into His Voice

My prayer for you as you read this book is that you would fully appreciate the gift that God has given you: ears to hear Him. God does want to speak to you, and in fact, He already does. He's not interested in speaking to you only through your pastor. In fact the Bible tells us that He speaks to us in various ways:

> **""For God speaks once, And even twice, yet no one notices it [including you, Job]. In a dream, a vision of the night [one may hear God's voice], When deep sleep falls on men while slumbering upon the bed, Then He opens the ears of men And seals their instruction."** *Job 33:14-16 (AMP)*.

This powerful truth reminds us that God speaks in different ways—through dreams, visions, and direct instructions—yet many fail to recognize His voice. You do not need to spend another moment in the camp of the spiritually deaf—it doesn't pay.

A major obstacle to hearing God is ulterior motives—serving Him with a hidden agenda. We are called to manifest God just as He is (1 John 4:17). That is why rebellion, manipulation, and covetousness have no place in this revival. Balaam is a perfect example—a man who appeared prayerful but coveted inwardly. Though God had clearly told him not to go with Balak's messengers, he prayed again, hoping for a different answer. God let him go—but it was against His will.

If you persist in wanting your own way, God may allow your desires—but the outcome will not be in your favor.

The quickest antidote to this obstacle is unconditional love. We must love God purely—desiring nothing but Him in all His holiness.

- No ulterior motives.

- No self-serving prayers.

- If God says "No," it remains a "No."

When He has already spoken in His Word, there is no need to pray for an alternative answer. God cannot lie, nor will He go against His Word.

That is why I am not fond of the song *Phindukhulume* in our native Siswati, which translates to "Speak again, Lord." While its intention may seem sincere, it is often misused by people who are dissatisfied with what God has already spoken. Instead of aligning their will with His, they sing this song hoping for a different answer.

Yet when God speaks, He does not waver or contradict Himself. His Word is final, and His nature unchanging.

"For I am the Lord, I do not change..." Malachi 3:6 (AMPC)

God is our loving Father, but He is also our God—He must be obeyed. While it is true that He is love, we must tremble before Him in reverence. God loves you: Don't disappoint Him! Don't disappoint Him! Don't disappoint Him! His plans for you are too great, and His love is too profound for you to settle for anything less than full obedience.

Hearing God's voice means nothing if you only obey when it suits you. Let us love Him enough to obey Him always.

Let us remind ourselves of some of what we covered.

- God speaks for our benefit.

- Spiritual deafness makes you a victim of deception

- His voice is our safety, success, and security.

- Obedience is not selective—if you truly love God, you will obey Him.

This is not the time to pray for revival while refusing to hear God. Revival is the promised land for those who listen and obey. My prayer for you as you read this is that your ability to hear God becomes clearer—that your spirit becomes attuned to His voice so that you may walk in full obedience to His will.

In the next chapter, we will explore the incredible things God has revealed—the power He is going to unleash, the glory that will descend upon the earth, and most importantly, His manifest presence among us. This revival is unlike anything seen before. But with great power comes great responsibility. We have a role to play, and the time to step into it is now.

Chapter Six

Great Power Comes with Great Responsibility

"Therefore, be on the alert [be prepared and ready], for you do not know the day nor the hour [when the Son of Man will come]."
Matthew 25:13 AMP

The great power that God is bringing to planet Earth will only be entrusted to those who prepare. In past moves of God, ministers of the gospel performed mighty miracles—even while some lived in compromise. Often, this was due to a lack of preparation ahead of the move of God. Unfortunately, this not only tainted people's understanding of His power, but many of these individuals failed to finish strong.

But this time, that will not be an option. And for two critical reasons:

First, God is bringing a holy power, and He intends to entrust it only to those who are ready—those who have prepared their hearts and lives to carry it. No one should be killed by the Glory. The vessels must be as pure as the power they carry.

Second, this revival will not end. Unlike past revivals that burned brightly for a season and then faded, this move of God will intensify until it ushers in the return of Christ. This means that those who are used in this season must remain holy, steadfast, and prepared to finish well. It is not enough to be used briefly—we must endure until the very end. If a person allows pride, sin, or compromise to creep in, they risk disqualification from the very revival they were called to carry. Worse still, they may fall away completely and miss the return of Christ.

This is why preparation is not optional. It is the qualifier for those who will be part of this great and final move of God.

Chosen for this Season

Before we discuss preparation, let us first reaffirm this truth: God has chosen us for this season. We are a privileged generation. Many before us fasted, prayed, and longed to see this day, but it is us who will walk in it. It is no accident that we are alive at this moment in history. God has a purpose for each of us, and He alone determines the times and seasons. Our responsibility is to prepare our hearts, minds, and lives to be vessels He can use in this end-time revival.

> **"For those whom He foreknew [and loved and chose beforehand], He also predestined to be conformed to the image of His Son [and ultimately share in His complete sanctification], so that He would be the firstborn [the most beloved and honored] among many believers. And those whom He predestined, He also called; and those whom He called, He also justified [declared free of the guilt of sin]; and those whom He justified, He also glorified [raising them**

to a heavenly dignity]." Romans 8:29-30 (AMP)

This is a great honor, but I want to balance it with humility. We did not choose this time—none of us sent a letter to God requesting to be born in this era. Yet, here we are. And while we had no say in the timing of our birth or the role we are called to play, we do have a responsibility: to ensure that God never regrets choosing us.

His decision to call us must not be in vain. This awareness should ignite a sense of urgency within us—we must prepare ourselves for the task ahead.

Why Prepare?

Throughout this book, we have seen that God's power comes with conditions: obedience and a willingness to hear His voice. Though it is God's desire to use available people, it is our responsibility to prepare ourselves. We must recognize that being chosen by God is both a privilege and an honor.

The stakes are high. As the Bible says, *to whom much is given, much is required.* (Luke 12:48 paraphrased)

God has granted us an extraordinary season of preparation, pouring out the greatest measure of revelation in human history. This means more will be required of us than of those who came before. This is both sobering and exciting because we are part of God's final move.

Believing the words of the prophets is not enough. Our response cannot simply be to clap, shout, or rejoice—we must prepare. When the world comes to witness what God is doing, they must not find us unready. They should never have to ask, *"Did these people not know we were coming?"*

Let us rise to the call and prepare ourselves for this great and final harvest. Because God holds those who have received greater revelation to a higher standard. He does not treat ignorance and knowledge the same way. Consider the Philistines—they placed the Ark of the Covenant on a cart hitched on two milk cows (1 Samuel 6:10), and God honored it. But when the Israelites tried to do the same thing, it resulted in death.

Why? Because the Israelites had been given knowledge of God's ways and were expected to uphold His instructions with reverence. We cannot afford to be careless with what we have received. This is not the time to take God's revelation lightly. It is time to prepare.

It is an honor to be chosen, but it is also a responsibility. Let us not be like those who celebrate being chosen but fail to prepare.

Learning from the Regent King

Let me share an example to emphasize the responsibility we carry. Throughout history, there have been moments when a king dies, leaving a young heir to assume the throne. Infact, Henry IV was 8 months old when he was crowned King. This heir is left with no choice but to grow up quickly, unlike other boys his age. From the moment he is crowned, his life dramatically changes.

While other boys play soccer in the streets, his childhood is set aside. Instead of carefree games, he must now learn to rule. He begins rigorous training—learning how to carry himself as a king, speak with authority, and bear the weight of responsibility. Unlike his peers, he can no longer live for himself; his focus must shift to the well-being of the kingdom entrusted to him.

In the same way, we too have been chosen. Not as rulers of earthly kingdoms, but as kings and priests in a far greater Kingdom—the Kingdom of God. It may seem surprising, especially given what the world has told you about yourself, but I say to you today: You are a king. Jesus Christ, our elder brother, is the King of kings, and we are called to reign with Him.

> **"And hast made us unto our God kings and priests: and we shall reign on the earth."** *Revelations 5: 10 (KJV)*

Just as the young heir must prepare for his throne, we too must prepare to carry the weight of this divine responsibility. This means separating ourselves for the purpose of the end-time revival, turning fully to God, and learning from Him how to carry this great move forward. We cannot leave like others.

You are not ordinary. You have been called, justified, and given the authority to reign with Christ. But with great authority comes great responsibility. Let us prepare accordingly.

Preparing for Revival

By now, I hope you fully grasp how incredible this revival will be and the privilege we have of being chosen to be part of it. I also hope you now clearly understand why preparation is absolutely necessary.

As we have mentioned before, this is the first revival where God has shared as much information as He has. That alone tells us that the stakes are high.

Now, let us discuss key ways we must prepare ourselves for this revival. This is not an exhaustive list—some aspects, such as hearing God and the formation of Christ in man, will be covered in greater depth in other chapters. God has spoken about the formation of Christ for many years because only Christ can carry the glory—we, in our own human constitution and nature, cannot.

For this chapter, we will focus on two major aspects of preparation:

1. **Understanding the time we live in and its demands.**

2. **Understanding the power and authority that God has released.**

Demands of the Time

To illustrate the importance of timing, imagine an athletics race. Before the race begins, the athletes warm up, take their positions, and listen carefully for the umpire's instructions:

"On your marks, get set, ready, go!"

It is absolutely critical that the athletes hear and respond at the right moment. Now imagine an athlete who stays on "your marks" when the umpire has already said "Go!" That athlete has already lost the race.

In the same way, we must understand the time we are living in. The trumpet has already sounded. God has declared that this is the final and greatest revival. Precision and obedience are vital. We cannot afford to move ahead of the Holy Spirit, nor can we afford to lag behind. We must move exactly when He tells us to move.

For years, God has been speaking about this revival. Many of us have heard these prophetic words, but hearing alone does not qualify us to be part of this move of God. If we fail to prepare, we risk standing on the sidelines as spectators, watching what God is doing through others.

God is not looking for those who heard about the revival first; He is looking for those who are available, surrendered, and ready to act. The people He will use in this time will not be distracted by applause, positions, or recognition—their sole focus will be fulfilling God's call in this last and greatest revival. Let us prepare ourselves for the demands of this time.

Power and Authority

The second key area of preparation is understanding the power and authority that the Lord has released in this time. This power and authority, which come through the Holy Spirit, the Man of the Hour, will be absolutely vital in this season. The Lord Jesus told us in His Word that when we receive the Holy Spirit, we also receive power. If you have received Him, you already have the power.

But let us take a moment to clarify what this power truly is. The power we are talking about is holy power. It cannot be faked. It cannot be counterfeited by deceivers. It is not something you can obtain from an evil witch doctor, like the wolves today, and then try to fool the people of God.

This power comes only from the Holy Spirit.

Here is an important truth: This power is not dependent on age or gender—it is activated by faith. The Holy Spirit empowers us, but faith is the channel that allows that power to work. Without faith, unbelief can render a person powerless, causing them to live and die without ever having used the power within them.

Now, I realize that we often use the words power and authority interchangeably, but they are actually not the same.

- Power is an irresistible force that drives back the enemy. When power operates, it pushes back the evil forces.

- Authority is not about force—it is about standing in a position of rightful command. That is why we should not be found in an illegitimate position.

To illustrate the difference, consider this example: a person with power can physically push a car—that is power at work. But a police officer, without physical strength, can command a driver to stop the car. Why? Because the officer operates in authority. They have the legal right to give orders. And while a nurse has authority in a hospital, they do not have authority in ordering traffic to move. Position matters!

Here are the good news: we have both power and authority. The authority the Lord Jesus received when He rose from the dead has been given to us as well. In case you didn't know, this is the scale of the power and authority that has been given to you:

> **"Jesus approached and, breaking the silence, said to them, 'All authority (all power of rule) in heaven and on earth has been given to Me.'"** *Matthew 28:18 (AMPC)*

The Only Question is: Do We Know We Have it?

The devil thrives on the ignorance of the Church. But when we understand our power and authority, we will walk in the fullness of our calling.

The Call to Prepare

This is the greatest time in God's calendar for the Church. No matter how things may appear, I want you to know that the best is yet to come for the Church. But we must be ready—fully prepared to step into our role and be part of this great move of God.

Let us use this time wisely to prepare, ensuring that we are not scrambling to get ready during the revival itself. Let no cracks be found in us because the glory of God will expose those cracks. Now is the time to fortify our hearts, align ourselves with His will, and take the call of preparation seriously. This is not a season to take lightly—it is a season to rise.

The athletes have already been positioned. The trumpet has sounded. The call has gone out. This is not a time to hesitate or procrastinate. We cannot afford to stand still. We must move with God! And the only way to move with God is to prepare. Let us get ourselves ready so that we do not find ourselves unqualified for the very revival we have been called to carry.

In the next chapter, we look at the experience we had in Pongola as a guide on how this power is released, how it transforms lives, and how it draws the world to Him. What we experienced in Pongola is a small picture of the great explosion of power that will come in this end-time revival.

Chapter Seven

Phongola: A Foretaste of Revival

During our month of fasting in June 1992, God prophesied through me that He was going to move mightily in Pongola, KwaZulu-Natal, South Africa. At the time, we were already in the area for a month of fasting and prayer, so we naturally assumed that God's move would happen immediately. However, the fulfillment of that prophetic word came three years later—a reminder that God's timing is not always our timing.

Preparation in Prayer

As you know by now, before anything of God happens, His people must pray. Holding onto that prophetic word, we began to pray earnestly, preparing for what God had promised. At the time, our church had only one branch—Madlangemphisi Miracle Centre. When God first called me to ministry, He instructed me to name all our branches "Miracle Centres" because they would be places where

He would perform miracles, signs, and wonders.

Our prayers for this move began in Madlangemphisi, a rural town in the Hhohho region of Eswatini. Looking back, most of what we did there was prayer. We did not just pray—we lived in and enjoyed the presence of God. The more we prayed for Pongola, the deeper God drew us into intercession. It was a beautiful and relentless cycle—prayer leading to more prayer, drenching us in His presence.

As a church, we prayed corporately, believing God for the mighty move He had promised. We went as far as sending people ahead to Pongola to intercede and prepare the ground spiritually. While they prayed in Pongola, we continued to pray in Madlangemphisi. The spiritual momentum built like a tidal wave.

Revival Breaks Out

Finally, in 1995, we went to Pongola and began hosting tent services. God even showed us exactly where to place the tent. It was not the most glamorous or safest location, but one thing was certain—God moved mightily.

As we preached the Word, many people received Jesus Christ as their personal Lord and Savior. Many were baptized in the Holy Spirit, and countless testimonies emerged. People were being healed of all kinds of diseases. I often say that the only disease we did not see cured was leprosy—simply because no one had it!

Every time we gathered, the Glory of God descended upon the place. In many ways, Pongola felt like a foretaste of the coming end-time revival. It was a glimpse—a powerful preview—of the miracles, outpouring, and mighty works of God that will sweep across the earth in these last days.

Our time in Pongola reinforced an unshakable truth—God always honors His Word. All we need to do is believe. This season challenged and strengthened our faith, showing us firsthand that when God speaks, His Word never fails.

Overflow of Miracles

One unforgettable miracle involved a young man who was known in the area as being crippled. He had never attended any of the tent services during the crusade, so none of us knew him. But one night, God visited him in a vision.

In the vision, he saw me praying for him, and he was instructed to come and request prayer. He obeyed. He walked into the tent with deep conviction, shared the vision, and said, *"I am here now; please pray for me so I can walk just like you."*

Moved by his faith, we began to pray for him, and after prayer, he received his miracle—he walked! Many were astonished, including members of our own crusade team. In fact, for some of them, it was the longest night of their lives—they could hardly wait for morning to check if the young man was still walking.

As word spread, people flocked to see for themselves. Would the boy still be healed? Praise God—he was! The power of God is real, and it is holy.

Yet, as is often the case, some doubted. They scoffed, saying, "Once the tent leaves, he will stop walking." But God's power is not temporary, nor is it confined to a specific location. We have returned to Pongola many times since then—and every time, we have found him still walking!

When news of the miracles began to spread, people came from far and wide. In addition to the local crowds, some traveled all the way from Johannesburg—over 400 kilometers away, making a 4 to 5-hour journey just to bring their loved ones for healing. It was a glimpse of how this end-time revival will unfold. As I explained earlier, the initial explosion of God's power will draw people to see for themselves, and what they witness will ignite even greater outpourings.

In Pongola, we saw all manner of miracles. People stood up from wheelchairs, years of affliction vanished, and God remained faithful to His Word. As the testimonies spread, people no longer waited for the tent meetings. Instead, they sought us out—gathering at the house where we stayed. Each morning, before we even set foot at the tent, we would wake up to find multitudes already waiting.

One unforgettable morning, before we had even left the house, a young girl was brought to us—lifeless.

She was dead.

Her still body was laid in my arms. We began to pray, and by the grace of God, He raised her from the dead!

When word of this miracle spread, the crowds exploded. For weeks, families carried their sick and afflicted to us. Each morning, our yard was filled with people, waiting for prayer. And God, ever faithful to His Word, continued to heal—not because of us, but because they came with faith.

Lessons from Pongola

Our time in Pongola was rich with lessons, many of which deepened our understanding of what it takes to be effective in revival. One of the most significant lessons was the power of unity among brethren.

The unity and love in our team were palpable, demonstrated not just in words, but in action and sacrifice. An example that I touched on earlier is that while some of our brethren prayed in Madlangemphisi, Eswatini, others were praying in Pongola, South Africa. Some team members even slept in the crusade tent because they were praying until sleep overtook them. This spirit of unity in prayer created an environment where God's power could flow mightily.

We already understood the importance of prayer. Beyond the main services, we held dedicated prayer sessions to sustain the move of God. However, as the crowds increased and the demand for miracles grew, our time became stretched. People would even show up where we were staying. Soon, it became difficult to hold prayer sessions consistently. The sheer volume of people needing healing took our focus, and prayer started to take a back seat. Eventually, the wave of God's presence lifted, and the tent campaign came to an end.

This was a critical lesson: prayer is everything in revival. As great as God's move in Pongola was, it was only a glimpse of what is coming in this end-time revival. The level of prayer required to sustain what God is about to do must be even greater. That means our preparation for revival should include a plan for how we will maintain prayer, at both an individual and corporate level. What we experienced in Pongola was a foretaste—a shadow of the magnitude of God's plans for this generation.

We must grasp this truth: when God moves, there must be people ready to pray. Without sustained prayer, revival will not last. I recently told some of our brethren at church this lesson, do everything in your power to maintain what triggered your breakthrough—in our case it was prayer.

In the next chapter, we will dive deeper into the importance of prayer—how it prepares the ground, sustains God's movement, and keeps us aligned with His will.

Pongola taught us one undeniable truth: Prayer is what sustains the move of God.

Chapter Eight

Prayer is the Engine for Revival

"**E**lias was a man subject to like passions as we are, and he prayed earnestly that it might not rain: and it rained not on the earth by the space of three years and six months."
James 5: 17 KJV

The greatest lesson we took from our time in Pongola is this: revival cannot be sustained without prayer. No matter how powerfully God moves, prayer must never stop. Revival does not eliminate the need for prayer; rather, it intensifies it. The first signs of revival should not lead to contentment but to even greater intercession.

As we discuss this chapter, I hope and pray that you fully grasp the necessity of prayer in sustaining revival. We will highlight historical and biblical examples of persistent intercession. Others have done it before, which means you can do it too.

Prayer is absolutely essential. I do not really give out "steps to success." If someone were to ask me about the seven steps to success, my answer would be clear: the first step is prayer, the second step is prayer, the third is prayer, and so on, all the way to the seventh—prayer. As Christians, our success begins and ends with prayer.

The Indispensable Role of Prayer in Revival

God has declared that this end-time revival will move from wave to wave, growing in intensity and impact. However, for this to happen, we must sustain it through continual prayer. Without prayer—whether in our personal lives or as a church—we cannot and will not see the full extent of what God wants to do in this generation.

When we say that prayer is the engine of revival, we mean it. Everything that happens in a car is driven by its engine—its strength, its health, and its maintenance determine the car's performance. A car cannot function without an engine, and the engine is one of the most costly investments in a vehicle. This is why prayer is essential to revival. It is not just an accessory or a preliminary step—it is the power source that keeps the revival moving forward. Without prayer, revival will not last.

When we discussed the properties of revival earlier, I shared a vision in which I saw prayers being offered all over Eswatini before the revival broke out. It was a reminder that revival is always preceded by prayer. This will not be unique to us, but rather a blueprint for revival. Some historians recount that the Welsh Revival was preceded by prayer groups formed across the nation, interceding for revival before it came. And they saw exactly what they were praying for. The Azusa Street Revival also followed this same pattern. If you visit the Bonnie Brae House today, it stands as a testimony to the people who gathered there and prayed until revival came.

This is why prayer is the engine. It does not just ignite revival—it sustains it. Without prayer, revival cannot be birthed, and without sustained prayer, revival will not last. Revival has a price, and that price is unceasing, sacrificial prayer. Every great move of God has been birthed and sustained by intercessors who refused to stop praying.

God has promised us revival, but we must pray it into reality. If we desire to see this great and final move of God, then we must be willing to take on the responsibility of prayer. This is not the time for casual prayers—it is the time for persistent, fervent, and unrelenting intercession.

Revival will come, but it will come through those who are willing to pay the price in prayer.

Answered Prayer

Prayer is the key that unlocks much of what God desires to do in this season. And the amazing thing about prayer—something I hope many will begin to understand—is that when we pray the prayers God desires of us, prayer becomes an easy task. Why? Because the One who gives us the prayer is the same One answering the prayer on the other side. This is the simplest and most effective way to pray—praying in alignment with what God wants us to pray. When our prayers are in sync with His will, there is no striving. We are merely partnering with heaven's agenda, allowing God's desires to be fulfilled through us.

We must be open to learning the ways of prayer. Even the disciples had to ask the Lord Jesus, "Lord, teach us how to pray." This tells us that prayer is something we learn and grow in. As we yield to God and learn to pray according to His will, we will see greater results and deeper intimacy with Him. Let me share some keys to answered prayer that I pray will assist you in your journey of prayer.

One of the most critical principles of prayer is that it requires both submission and persistence—submission to God's will and persistence until what He desires is accomplished. Prayer is not about imposing our will on God—it is about aligning ourselves with His will. We must be willing to set aside personal desires—even pressing needs—and align ourselves with God's priorities. The Bible reminds us that we often do not even know what to pray for, but the Holy Spirit does.

> **"In the same way, the Spirit helps us in our weakness. We do not know what we ought to pray for, but the Spirit Himself intercedes for us through wordless groans."** Romans 8: 26 (NIV)

Many people pray persistently, yet their prayers remain unanswered because they have not fully submitted to God's desires.

The Lord teaches us this lesson in the parable of the persistent widow who continually approached a wicked judge asking for justice (Luke 18: 1 - 8). The judge, though unjust, eventually granted her request because of her persistence. If even an unrighteous judge responds to persistence, how much more will our righteous God answer when His people persevere in prayer?

Another common mistake we make is sacrificing accuracy in prayer for quantity. Many believe they need to pray for everything, but this is not always the case. Let me tell you this: if God gives you one specific thing to pray about, focus on it. Zoom in on that one assignment and pray with precision. It is far better to pray accurately than to scatter prayers everywhere. This is especially important in this season of revival because God will be giving specific assignments in prayer. If we are faithful in those assignments, our role in the revival will be fulfilled. Revival will come, but it requires a level of sacrifice.

Let me share a testimony that illustrates this principle. There was a woman in our church to whom God gave specific things to pray for. However, at one point, her children began facing serious struggles, and she felt burdened to pray for them. But here is the important part: God had never instructed her to intercede for them.

In her distress, she decided to climb the mountains and intercede for them. (For those unfamiliar, in certain parts of the world, it is common for people to go to the mountains when seeking deep, uninterrupted time in prayer). She prayed and prayed, but God did not answer her prayer. And the truth is, that was not the assignment God had given her.

What she did not know was that God had already raised others to intercede for her children's restoration. Interestingly, when she refocused on what God had originally assigned her to pray for, the prayers of those interceding for her children were answered. Her children returned home and turned back to God!

This testimony serves as a powerful reminder:

- We must pray for what God has told us to pray for.

- Revival will be birthed when our prayers align with God's will.

- If we remain faithful to our assignments—no matter how large or small—God will move powerfully.

Prayer becomes easier when we live in holiness. A consecrated life produces effective prayers. We must return to prayer—not just occasional prayer, but persistent, unrelenting intercession. We must pray until what God has promised comes to pass.

When God called me to ministry, He gave our church—Revival Life Ministry—five pillars: Prayer, the Word, Praise and Worship, Holiness, and the Holy Spirit and His operations. Though these pillars have distinct roles, they are not separate from one another. They are interconnected, working together to sustain revival. As God revealed: a holy life begets prayer, and prayer begets a holy life. Together, a life of holiness and prayer will give birth to true worship. We cannot overlook worship in revival, but true worship must flow out of lives rooted in holiness and prayer.

The key for every believer is this:
- Live in holiness.

- Worship the Lord in spirit and in truth.

- Maintain a life of persistent and unrelenting prayer.

The Price of Prayer

The reality is that a life of prayer is costly, but we must be willing to pay the price. Throughout history, those who labored in prayer paid a price but they also saw the undeniable move of God. Consider John Hyde, a man who moved to India and became known as the Praying Apostle or simply Praying Hyde. Burdened for the nation, he consistently cried out to God to move in a way that had never been seen before. His intercession was so intense that it was said to have physically affected him. He formed the Punjab Prayer Union which prayed daily for half a day, for the conversion of souls[1].

And what followed his prayer? A mighty move of God.

In his final days, a doctor discovered that Hyde's heart had shifted from its natural position due to his unceasing posture of prayer. The doctor warned him that unless he changed his ways, he had only a few months to live. But Hyde continued to pray, and instead of dying, he lived several more years beyond the doctor's diagnosis.

This is a reminder that there is a price to prayer. But when we pray, God backs it up. We will discuss paying the price of prayer in subsequent chapters. But for now I want you to know that the cost looks different for each person. I remember in the early days in Madlangemphisi, there was a young girl who, despite our persistent prayers, did not receive the baptism of the Holy Spirit. She came for prayer repeatedly, and though others received, she did not. But then she made the a decision to fast.

Then one day on her way to the river to collect water, she was filled with the Spirit. As we were walk to the tent for our afternoon services, we heard someone flowing in the spirit inside. Wondering who had showed up before us, we found her filled with the Holy Spirit and praying fervently. She had paid her price for prayer.

This is an important lesson. Sometimes, the cost of breakthrough is not as grand as we imagine—but it requires obedience to what God asks of us.

Another price of prayer—one we discussed earlier—is alignment with God's will. This requires us to overlook our own desires and submit fully to what God wants. Many people struggle in prayer because they pray outside of God's will, focusing on personal desires rather than heaven's agenda. You may be wondering whether Simelane has exhausted his stories on prayer. The truth is, I have not. Just as James reminds us that Elijah was a man like us, I want you to see these stories as testimonies of ordinary people who encountered God through prayer. Let me share another example.

There was a woman in the early days of our ministry whom we prayed with often. Whenever we gathered to pray, she would remain silent for a long time before speaking.

At first, some wondered why.

But when she finally opened her mouth to pray, it was a marvel to witness. Her prayers were powerful, sharp, and filled with the presence of God. She had attained the secret of waiting on God—listening first before speaking. She refused to rush into prayer, instead waiting to understand what God wanted her to pray for. Then, once she knew, she would chase after it with full focus, bringing success to her intercession.

Another price to prayer is unity. Unity is not just a buzzword—it is a precondition for sustaining any move of God. Without it, revival cannot be maintained. While an individual prayer life is vital, corporate prayer is equally essential. Throughout His teachings, the Lord Jesus emphasized the principle of agreement in prayer. When we pray in agreement—not just with our mouths, but with our hearts—God answers those prayers. As we prepare for this end-time revival, we must guard the unity of prayer and ensure that prayer itself becomes a hallmark of our unity. Revival will not rest upon a divided people. The Holy Spirit is especially sensitive to unity. Where there is disunity, the power and presence of God cannot flow as intended.

One of the greatest things about prayer is that it invites God to dwell among us. When heartfelt prayer is offered, the presence of God descends and abides in that place. We had the privilege of experiencing this during the 1980s and 90s, in the early days of our ministry in Madlangemphisi. The intensity of our corporate prayers and the deep unity among us brought about undeniable moves of God. The glory of God would fill the entire place. His presence was so tangible that it extended far beyond the prayer center.

Some people testified that as they approached Madlangemphisi from kilometers away, they began to feel a shift in the atmosphere—a change brought about by the resting presence of God's glory. This divine atmosphere was made possible through fervent and consistent prayer. I pray that in our time, you and I may see again.

Lord, do it again!

Contending for Our Nations in Prayer

One of the greatest misunderstandings people have when we talk about the marvelous things God will do in this time is the assumption that the devil will simply fold his arms and enjoy the show. That could not be any further from the truth.

Yes, God is going to move powerfully, but the enemy will also work tirelessly to sabotage what God is doing. However, his failure is guaranteed—because when the Lord's Word has gone forth, nothing can stop it from being fulfilled.

Even in this time of revival, we must contend in prayer for our nations. This revival is not just about personal transformation; it is about national and global transformation. God desires to see His power, His justice, and His righteousness sweep through every nation. To accomplish this, our prayers must be committed, unwavering, and fervent.

Our prayers can be so committed that we become reference points for intercession. In the book of Jeremiah, God uses Moses and Samuel as examples of powerful intercessors—individuals whose prayers moved heaven and shaped history:

> **"Even though Moses and Samuel were to stand before Me [interceding for them], My heart would still not be [turned with favor] toward this people [Judah]. Send them away from My presence and out of My sight and let them go!"** Jeremiah 15:1 (AMP)

This verse highlights the weight of prayer and the influence of faithful intercessors who stood in the gap for their people. One of the saddest verses in the Bible for me is when God looked for a man to stand in the gap and couldn't find even one.

The Bible tells us:

> **"I searched for a man among them who would build up the wall and stand in the gap before Me for [the sake of] the land, that I would not destroy it, but I found no one [not even one]."** Ezekiel 22:30 (AMP)

Even today, God is looking for men and women who will intercede for their nations. Revival is for every nation—but it must be contended for through prayer.

Will you stand in the gap? Will you pray for your nation? Will you contend in the spirit until revival breaks forth?

One of the most remarkable examples of national intercessions in the Bible is by Abraham. We see Abraham standing before God, pleading for mercy for Sodom and Gomorrah. He dared to speak to God, which is what prayer is, and he negotiated with Him:

> **"Will You indeed sweep away the righteous with the wicked? Suppose there are fifty righteous people within the city; will You indeed sweep it away and not spare the place for the sake of the fifty righteous who are in it?"** Genesis 18:23-24 (NASB)

Abraham started by asking God to spare the city for fifty righteous people. With boldness, he continued to press in, negotiating all the way down to ten righteous people. I often wonder why he stopped at ten—could he not have gone down to two? Perhaps he assumed that surely ten righteous people would be found within Lot's family.

Regardless, the lesson remains clear: Through prayer, we can move the heart of God—even in moments of national judgment. In this time of revival, prayer will not only usher in the supernatural but will also shift the political destinies of nations if we intercede faithfully.

Another powerful example of contending in prayer is seen with Elijah. Apostle James reminds us that Elijah was just a man like us—an ordinary man who submitted himself to prayer until the heavens obeyed. Elijah's example shows us that ordinary men and women can submit themselves to persistent prayer and shift natural and spiritual realities.

A more recent example of someone who contended for his nation through prayer was John Knox. Knox was one of the leaders of the Protestant Reformation in Scotland. At a time when his country had turned away from God, he famously prayed:

"Give me Scotland, or I die!"

In fact, Queen Mary of the Scots, a known opponent of Knox, was overheard in her palace saying:

" I fear the prayers of John Knox more than all the assembled armies of Europe"

Prayer is the key that will unlock much of what God desires to do in this season. If we desire to see revival in our nations, we must be willing to fight for it in prayer. This truth remains today:

- The devil will not hand our nations back to us on a silver platter.

- He will not surrender our cities unless we intercede.

- He will not surrender our families unless we pray.

The Garment of Prayer: Divine Empowerment for the Season

As we have discussed throughout this book, God does not leave things to chance, nor does He call us without equipping us. In this season of revival, He has promised to clothe His people with a garment of prayer. He will empower them to pray in ways they never could before—prayers that will shift atmospheres, bring breakthroughs, and accelerate His divine agenda on the earth.

I once had an experience that demonstrated this divine empowerment during a tent campaign in Eswatini. The meetings had been running for an entire week, but we were not seeing the results we were accustomed to.

On Sunday night, my last night before returning to work, I began praying for people to receive the Holy Spirit. But nothing happened. No movement. No breakthrough. We pressed on, praying and contending, but the resistance remained. Then, as I stood praying, I suddenly turned toward the wall. And in that moment, I felt something descend upon me—an invisible yet tangible garment. It was a shift in the spirit. Instantly, God began to move powerfully.

People were slain under the power of the Holy Spirit. Some were so overcome that they had to be carried home. What had taken days of struggle broke in mere moments. It was not because of my own strength—it was the power of divine empowerment.

This garment of prayer is God's gift to His people in this revival. He has assured us that this supernatural mantle will descend upon many—enabling them to pray for things that would ordinarily take years to pray for and they'll achieve breakthroughs in mere seconds or minutes.

This divine empowerment will accelerate the work of God. It will enable us to accomplish in a short time, what would otherwise take decades. It is a supernatural enablement to pray, to intercede, and to birth the purposes of God on the earth.

Revival Cannot Outgrow its Foundation of Prayer

Yet, as powerful as this garment of prayer will be, none of this can happen unless we pray. The truth is this: revival cannot grow beyond the prayers we offer. Just as a building cannot outgrow its foundation, revival cannot outgrow its foundation of prayer.

In the next chapter, we will explore a deeper truth—the importance of dying to oneself. As mentioned earlier, when God revealed the great things He planned to do in my life and through me, He also made one thing clear: I had to die to my own will and to the desires of my flesh.

This is the same journey our Lord Jesus walked in the Garden of Gethsemane. Before He could fulfill His mission, He had to confront His own will and surrender fully to the Father. If we are to carry this revival, we must come to that same place of complete surrender.

Revival cannot coexist with self-centeredness. It will require death to self and total submission to the purposes of God.

Chapter Nine

Dying to Self

> *"I am crucified with Christ: nevertheless I live; yet not I, but Christ liveth in me: and the life which I now live in the flesh I live by the faith of the Son of God, who loved me, and gave himself for me."*
> **Galatians 2:20 KJV**

In 1986, God was speaking to me. It was a wonderful day—one filled with His voice, His presence, and His promises. God spoke many things to me, many good things. I was overwhelmed with excitement as He revealed what He was going to do through my life. My heart was full of joy.

Then He said:

"But"

Before He even spoke the next words, I could sense that what was coming would not be comfortable for me.

"But you must die."

Die to self. Die to the flesh. Die to your own will. Die to your desires.

This was not a suggestion. It was a requirement. By "dying to self,"

He was not referring to physical death or acts like homicide or suicide. Instead, He was calling for a deliberate surrender of our will, our desires, and our fleshly ambitions. The weight of those words settled in my spirit. I knew this was not something I would naturally want. Yet, I also knew that if I desired to see the fulfillment of what He had spoken, I had to surrender. I had to embrace His call, no matter the cost.

This dying to self is not forced upon us; it is a choice. This surrender is necessary to accomplish what God wants to do during the revival.

If we were to equate this to a modern corporate environment, imagine that God was posting a job opening for those He would use in this end-time revival. One of the key qualifications would read:

"A person who has died to self."

Without question, this is a defining criterion for those who will participate in the greatest move of God in history.

The problem we see in much of the Church today is that many want revival without surrender. Many want power without consecration. Many want to be used by God while still clinging to the flesh.

A Surrendered Church

There are consequences to a church that is not dead to itself. When we look at the Church today and reflect on many of the issues that plague the Body of Christ, we can trace much of the turmoil back to a failure to die to self.

- Backbiting stems from self-interest.

- Gossip thrives in those who are still alive in the flesh.

- Rebellion and division are rooted in the unwillingness to submit to God's order.

Often, people try to justify themselves by saying, "I didn't do it first—they did it to me." But I must ask: If you were to strike a dead person, would they respond? No. If you insulted them, would they retaliate? No.

Because they are dead.

And that is the place we must reach in our own lives—where we are so surrendered to Christ that no offense can shake us, no persecution can move us, and no personal ambition can take us off course.

That is the kind of vessel God is seeking—one that has truly died to self. A vessel that, when God calls and commissions it, will simply obey without hesitation.

In Joel chapter 2, the prophet speaks of the last army—a unified and disciplined group of soldiers walking in total obedience to the orders of their Commander.

- They march forward without breaking rank.

- They do not interfere with another's assignment.

- They do not operate with "I" at the center.

Their strength comes from complete submission to the will of their Commander.

> **"They run like mighty men; they climb the wall like men of war. They march each one [straight ahead] on his ways, and they do not break their ranks. Neither does one thrust upon another; they walk every one in his path. And they burst through and upon the weapons, yet they are not wounded and do not change their course...And the Lord utters His voice before His army, for His host is very great, and [they are] strong and powerful who execute [God's] word.**

For the day of the Lord is great and very terrible, and who can endure it?" Joel 2: 7-8 & 11 (AMPC)

This is the last day's army, its strength comes from obedience. God desires to speak to His people and work through them, but at every turn, we must obey. I cannot overemphasize the importance of obedience in this revival. Obedience in revival demands a level of precision—it must be both timely and accurate.

This kind of obedience can only come from those who have truly died to all self. When the self is removed, there is no room for hesitation, doubt, or selective hearing. God requires vessels that are wholly surrendered, ready to follow His instructions without deviation or delay.

Scripture underscores the immense value God places on obedience. The level of obedience here comes down to timing and accuracy. Saul lost his kingship not because he refused to act, but because he failed to carry out the exact instruction of the Lord. Partial obedience is still disobedience. Revival cannot move forward with half-hearted obedience. If we are to be used in this great move of God, our obedience must be full, complete, and immediate. Our obedience must align with God's will.

"Has the Lord as great a delight in burnt offerings and sacrifices As in obedience to the voice of the Lord? Behold, to obey is better than sacrifice, and to heed [is better] than the fat of rams. For rebellion is as [serious as] the sin of divination (fortune-telling), and disobedience is as [serious as] false religion and idolatry. Because you have rejected the word of the Lord, He also has rejected you as king." 1 Samuel 15: 22-23 (AMP)

The reason I am harping on this is because God once taught us this: "Delayed obedience is not obedience." Our obedience must be timely. We must respond promptly as soon as God speaks. When we delay, we risk failing to accomplish what He has sent us to do. Furthermore, misguided obedience is no different from disobedience.

Obedience is critical in this revival—mark this: in all conditions. We cannot limit our obedience to moments of convenience or times when there is personal benefit. We must obey whenever God speaks! However, this level of obedience requires one thing: We must be completely dead to self. This is yet another reminder of how essential it is, in this end-time revival, to have died to our own desires and flesh.

Death to Self Enables Obedience

The more we die to ourselves, the more obedience becomes second nature. God's desires become our desires. Even our prayers will align more effortlessly with His will. We can confidently echo the words of the Apostle Paul to the Church in Galatia:

> **"It is no longer I who live, but Christ lives in me."**
> (Galatians 2:20)

But here is the truth: We cannot genuinely declare that Christ is the one living in us until we have died to our own will. Dying to all self, or all flesh is crucial. Some of the things God will do through us in this revival will demand tremendous faith, and the last thing we want is for our own will to stand in the way of what God wants to accomplish.

With all these being said, dying to self is not easy. In fact, it may be the hardest thing to do. But it is a requirement that even His Son, Jesus Christ, had to meet. In the Garden of Gethsemane, the human will of Christ broke, and from that moment forward, He fully surrendered to fulfilling the will of God. After praying to the point where His sweat was like drops of blood, the Lord uttered the most powerful prayer of surrender

> ***"Father, if You are willing, remove this cup [of divine wrath] from Me; yet not My will, but [always] Yours be done."*** Luke 22:42 (AMP)

If God required this of His Son, how much more does He require it of us?

This is a critical hour in history. God will use anyone willing to surrender their will. A dead person becomes a vessel fit to carry the Holy Spirit. As we said in the Holy Spirit: The Man of the Hour chapter, the presence of the Holy Spirit will only have significance in our lives if we are ready to obey Him. Obedience is what ushers in what God wants to accomplish. It is part of God's divine plan to dwell in us and be the one who works through us. But this can only be achieved if He is the sole authority living within us.

The Choice to Die to Self

Some of the things God will ask of us will be difficult, but we must be willing and ready to obey and manifest whatever He is doing. No one else can lay down your will for you. It is a personal and consequential decision, one that is not easy but necessary. Choosing to die to self means relinquishing control, and though the will of man is tough to break, it is essential for those who desire to carry God's power. In fact, breaking Jesus Christs' will as the Son of God was easier than breaking the will of man. Yet, dying to self opens the door to new life and multiplication. As He declared:

> **"I assure you and most solemnly say to you, unless a grain of wheat falls into the earth and dies, it remains alone [just one grain, never more]. But if it dies, it produces much grain and yields a harvest."**
> John 12:24 (AMP)

We can sing about surrender and even weep in prayer over it, but the act of truly laying down our will is another matter entirely. You must choose death. Once you choose death to self, you relinquish all personal rights. The vessel God is seeking in this time is one that will go wherever He wants and do whatever He commands.

A significant cause of delay in the Church's progress is this: We have not fully died to self. God must be the only one living in us. He cannot share us with ourselves. It is either Him or us—there is no middle ground. Everything God has spoken about this end-time revival will only come to pass when we die to self.

The hard truth is that no one else can make this decision for you. Sermons can inspire you, and teachings can guide you, but the act of dying to your own will must come from you. True transformation happens only when you make that choice.

The call to die to self is not something that comes naturally to us. In our human nature, we resist it. We want to hold on—to our desires, our plans, and our way of doing things. Dying to self and surrendering completely to God is not an easy path. But when you come to understand that this death is for your own good, your prayer must change. You must cry out to God for the strength to obey. You must ask Him to enable you to let go.

Dying to Self is the Foundation

Once the foundation is laid, there is a building process that must take place. God is raising a people who can carry Him. That is why God first spoke to us about dying to self before He could speak to us about the formation of Christ in man. We had to die to self so that Christ could be formed in us.

Only after this did He speak to us about **the Glory**—because only Christ can carry the Glory. The flesh cannot bear it. Self cannot sustain it. The Glory belongs to Christ alone, and for Him to dwell fully in us, we must first die.

This is God's divine order:

1. **Death to self** – Letting go of our will, our desires, and our ways.

2. **The formation of Christ** – Allowing Him to take shape in us, transforming us into His likeness.

3. **The Glory** – The manifestation of His presence and power, revealed only through Christ in us.

This is why surrender is necessary. It is the only way to become vessels fit for His glory. Throughout history, before every great move of God, there has always been a period of preparation—a divine building season where God works on His people, refining them, equipping them, and shaping them into vessels fit for His glory.

The next chapter will guide us in understanding what it means to be fully prepared for the extraordinary move of God.

Chapter Ten

It's Building Time in the Kingdom of God

"I fed you with milk, not solid food; for you were not yet able to receive it. Even now you are still not ready."
1 Corinthians 3:2 (AMP)

For far too long, the Church has been fed with milk—so much so that it has rotted their teeth. This has gone on for so long that when someone brings solid food, the people of God look at them strangely. The reason? They have not been built—they have been entertained.

But now, God is doing something different.

We are truly blessed to live in a time when God is actively preparing His people for the coming revival. This is a *season of building*—where He is shaping His Church to be ready for the great move ahead. It is certainly building time in the Kingdom of God!

Jesus Christ told a parable about ten virgins—five wise and five foolish (Matthew 25:1-13). The wise virgins were prepared with oil in their lamps, while the foolish ones were unprepared, assuming they had time. But when the bridegroom came, only those who were ready entered.

This is a warning to us.

- Revival is coming. Will we be prepared or left outside?

- God is calling. Will we be equipped or caught off guard?

- The time for spiritual immaturity is over. God is raising a people who are built to carry Him.

We must be found prepared and ready. God has chosen to equip us for this season, ensuring that we are *not caught off guard.*

Spiritual Building is by God's Design

Spiritual building is not a work of carnality. When building time comes upon the Church, God does not leave that to the design of man. Instead, He retains *full control over the design,* specifying what must be built, how it must be built, and where it must be built.

In fact, God does not use human ability to accomplish the divine; He has made this clear throughout history. When God is building, He provides very specific instructions—divine blueprints that must be followed precisely.

We see this pattern in Scripture:

- **Noah's Ark** – God gave Noah exact dimensions, materials, and even specified the gopher wood he had to use (Genesis 6:14-16). Noah could not alter or modify the design—he had to build exactly as God commanded.

- **The Tabernacle** – During the construction of the Tabernacle, God provided detailed specifications, down to the workers He called by name. In Exodus, He specifically mentions Bezalel:

> **"See, I have called by name Bezalel the son of Uri, the son of Hur, of the tribe of Judah. I have filled him with the Spirit of God in wisdom and skill, in understanding and intelligence, in knowledge, and in all kinds of craftsmanship."** Exodus 31:2-3 (AMP)

Even those who worked on sewing the curtains were not simply skilled seamstresses—they were divinely appointed and equipped by God to meet His exact specifications. He told Moses, **"See that you make them after the pattern for them, which was shown to you on the mountain."** Exodus 25:40 (NASB). This shows that God's divine order leaves no room for human improvisation.

In this time, God is building again, and He is doing so according to His divine specifications. This is not a time for human innovation but for total alignment with His plans. The specifications are critical because they reflect His purpose and Glory. We are in a building season in the Kingdom of God, and it is essential that we follow His instructions exactly as He reveals them.

Whenever God chooses to build, He assigns the man to build and retains the full autonomy over the designs. In the same way, in this season, we are called to align ourselves with God's blueprint—not our own ideas.

- The commissioned man cannot choose anything. He must hear everything from God.

- Church leaders and pastors today have the same responsibility. They cannot build God's people their own way—they must download from Mount Zion and build according to God's specifications.

The Church is not man's creation; it belongs to God and must be constructed with spiritual precision and accuracy. This is not a time to build casually or recklessly. We cannot afford to build God's people just anyhow.

The Importance of God's Divine Pattern

Before we discuss the laborers that the Lord is using to build the fivefold ministry, we must first understand why God builds according to a pattern. The truth is, God is building a brand-new man in our time. However, this might seem confusing because this "new man" is as old as eternity itself—God is building Himself inside His people. This new man is not an individual but a corporate man. Out of many, God is forming one—the Body of the Lord Jesus Christ. This Body is not just an assembly of believers; it is the Bride of the Lamb.

In the book of Revelation, we see an angel saying to John:

> **"Come, let me show you the wife of the Lamb."**
> Revelation 21:9 (AMP)

Yet, when John looked, he did not see the most beautiful woman in the universe; instead, he saw a city—a beautiful city descending from heaven, adorned as a bride for her husband. This means the Bride of the Lamb is a city—the City of the Living God. If this is true, then the process of building must be perfect. God is constructing His Church to be a structure that fully houses His presence and carries out His will in this final revival.

This building must be done precisely according to God's specifications. The main reason being that only the Lord Jesus can carry the

Glory that will be released in revival time. We will cover this in the next chapter. There are two additional operational reasons for the pattern:

1. Revival Requires a Collective Effort

The work of revival is too vast for one person to accomplish alone. Samson's story illustrates the necessity of collaboration. Though the anointing was upon Samson and not upon the foxes, the task demanded that Samson gather 300 foxes, set them in motion, and use them to accomplish something he could not have done alone in ten years.

> **"So Samson went and caught three hundred foxes, and took torches and turning the foxes tail to tail, he put a torch between each pair of tails."** Judges 15:4 (AMP)

This account demonstrates the power of mobilization. Samson understood that while the anointing was upon him, he needed a greater force to achieve God's purpose. In this end-time revival, God is raising an army, not individual superstars. Every believer has a role to play, and collective unity will produce far greater results than individual efforts. We must unify and labor together as one Body, ensuring that we follow God's instructions with humility and obedience. This unity is easier when we have been built according to the specifications of the Grand architect. He knows the graces he has inserted into each of us and how they can complement each other.

2. Revival Requires Generational Complementarity

God has spoken clearly that in this revival, He will use young people mightily, but they must rely on the wisdom of seasoned leaders. In fact, He said that the gray hair of the elders is an asset to the Church. This revival is not about a generational divide; it is about generational unity. The strength and passion of the youth must be balanced with the wisdom of the experienced to fulfill God's vision. We must not fall into the modern trend where the youth reject the wisdom of the elders, nor should elders fail to release the next generation into their calling. Just as Joshua could not step into leadership until Moses laid hands on him, the older generation must bless, equip, and release the younger generation to carry the torch forward. We should always remember: regardless of how many miracles one does, the one who is sent is never greater than the one who sent him. Consider this:

- Joshua saw many miracles and led Israel into Canaan, but he was not greater than Moses.

- Elisha performed twice as many miracles as Elijah, but he was not greater than Elijah.

This revival demands a unified effort. Every member of the Body of Christ has a role to play. Harmony and collective obedience will be the key to accomplishing the magnitude of what God is calling us to build. And only those who have been built by God will be willing to submit themselves to His divine plan and play their part in this great work.

The Renewing of the Fivefold Ministry

God is not just building, but he is also building the builders. As part of this rebuilding process, God is renewing and raising the Fivefold Ministry—apostles, prophets, evangelists, pastors, and teachers—to equip the saints for the work of ministry. The ministry is not confined to these roles, but rather, it is the responsibility of the entire Body of Christ. He did not set a pattern for preachers alone, but for every child of God. The Lord Jesus' life and ministry were not exclusive blueprints for Fivefold ministers; they serve as a call to action for all who follow Him.

God is renewing the Fivefold Ministry because it has been too focused on doing the work instead of equipping believers to carry it forward. Its purpose is not to centralize power but to empower the Body of Christ to fulfill its calling.

As part of this restoration, God is reviving the offices of Apostle and Prophet, which have been misrepresented. The title of Apostle has become a mere label, often assumed without Christ's anointing. True apostles are called by Him, not appointed by men or self-proclaimed. Many true apostles serve faithfully in the office of a pastor, while some who claim the title of apostle were never called by God in the first place. I remember being invited to an ordination service. I was told the man was to be ordained as a pastor. But just as I was about to pray, the Lord spoke to me clearly: "He is an apostle." So I ordained him into that office instead.

We must align with God's true callings—not human expectations or titles.

The prophetic office has also suffered great misrepresentation, particularly in our day. The enemy always seeks to introduce counterfeits before the genuine move of God, causing many to reject the truth. False prophets have infiltrated the Church in our time, leading some believers to distance themselves from prophecy altogether. Yet, the role of the prophet remains essential. A prophet's duty is to bring down revelation, to help the people of God know Him and understand His Word.

That is why the prophet is given a big ear—to hear God clearly and relay only what the Lord is saying, not what people want to hear. A prophet must reach a state of complete disinterest in personal ambition. He must have no personal agenda, no message of his own—only then can he faithfully serve as God's mouthpiece and contribute to building His people. If a prophet carries his own desires into ministry, he risks prophesying his own wishes rather than the will of God. The problem with this is that the prophet, not God, will then have to fulfill his words. We must reflect God alone, speaking only what He commands.

But God is renewing the office of the prophet. He is restoring it to its rightful place, raising prophets who will speak His Word in truth and righteousness. It is also important to understand that not everyone who prophesies stands in the office of a prophet, even if their prophecies are accurate. Accurate prophets recieve what is to come, as God does nothing without revealing it to His servants, the prophets (Amos 3:7)

As God renews the fivefold Ministry, we must embrace this restoration with humility, recognizing that this move is not about titles but about function. The work of equipping the saints is the priority, and as God rebuilds, we must align ourselves with His divine order.

Watch for Cracks in the Foundation

In the process of building, cracks sometimes appear in the foundation. They may start small, and inconspicuous, but if ignored, they weaken the structure over time. Left unchecked, these fractures can cause the entire building to collapse under pressure. Sin operates in the same way. If we do not radically confront and address every sin in our lives, it will fester and grow, ultimately leading to destruction.

Sin cannot be tolerated, even when it hides within us. Some only see sin as a problem when it appears in others, but we must hate sin in all forms, especially when it surfaces in our own hearts. The heart is our personal backyard, and we must tend to it with ruthless honesty and vigilance. If jealousy creeps in, do not wait until Sunday or for an altar call to seek God's mercy. Repent immediately. His grace is sufficient in every moment.

Take inventory of your heart regularly. Examine your thoughts, emotions, and relationships. Ask yourself:

- *Am I in secret competition with others?*

- *Can I genuinely rejoice when my brother prospers?*

- *If my fellow minister's church grows to 5,000 members while mine remains at 50, can I still dance and praise the Lord for him?*

If the answer is no, search your heart and ask why. These moments of self-examination expose hidden pride, envy, and the silent fractures that weaken our spiritual foundation.

One of the saddest things I have ever heard was of a prophet who refused to prophesy to others because he did not like them. Imagine withholding a word from the Lord because of personal feelings! Never take anything for granted. In this season of preparation, we must be unyielding and unkind to anything that could destroy us tomorrow. God is refining us. Our role is to cooperate fully—surrendering every weakness for His transforming power.

One of the most dangerous hindrances to fulfilling God's plan is pride. Pride and envy are subtle but destructive forces. If they begin to fester in your heart, be swift to confront them before they grow into something greater. I often say that pride is the deadliest weapon in the enemy's arsenal. Why? Because, unlike other sins that require pursuit, pride comes to you.

For example, for a person to commit adultery, they must seek out another individual. Theft requires an opportunity. But pride? Pride does not wait to be invited—it approaches you. It creeps into the heart unnoticed, disguising itself as self-importance, entitlement, or comparison. I always remind people: the devil did not commit fornication in heaven, nor did he steal money. The sin that caused him to be cast out was pride. Because he fell victim to it, he understands its destructive nature and wields it as his weapon of choice against us.

That is why we must humble ourselves. A man who is already humble cannot fall. Every great downfall, every spiritual collapse, began with pride. That is why the Bible warns:

> **"Pride goes before destruction, and a haughty spirit before a fall."** Proverbs 16:18 (AMP)

To guard against pride, we must seek humility. And our greatest example is the Lord Jesus Christ. Humility will be a cornerstone of this revival. The Bible commands us to be like the Christ, the ultimate example of humility:

> **"Have this same attitude in yourselves which was in Christ Jesus [look to Him as your example in selfless humility], who, although He existed in the form and unchanging essence of God [as One with Him, possessing the fullness of all the divine attributes-the entire nature of deity], did not regard equality with God a thing to be grasped or asserted [as if He did not already possess it, or was afraid of losing it]; but emptied Himself [without renouncing or diminishing His deity, but only temporarily giving up the outward expression of divine equality and His rightful dignity] by assuming the form of a bond-servant, and being made in the likeness of men [He became completely human but was without sin, being fully God and fully man]."** Philippians 2:5-7 (AMP)

His humility is a mystery so profound we may never fully grasp this side of heaven. To understand even a glimpse of what it meant for Him to humble Himself, I think of my childhood in rural Eswatini. Back then, we didn't have toys or electronics to keep us entertained; we made our own. Using clay, we molded cars, tractors, or cows.

Now, imagine becoming one of those clay figures we created—the creator becoming the creation. That is what the Lord Jesus did when He took on human form. It was a staggering act of humility, leaving His divine Glory to become one of us. This is why God the Father loves Him so dearly. The Lord Jesus didn't just give up His status; He became the benchmark of humility.

God is refining us, and we must cooperate fully by surrendering every weakness to His transforming power. The ultimate goal is to mature into true sons of God, just like our elder Brother, Jesus Christ.

Building of Sons

To walk in true humility, we must grow into spiritual maturity—transitioning from spiritual immaturity into sonship. This is crucial in this building time because God is not just preparing individuals; He is building sons.

The Apostle Paul explains this in Romans 8:

> **"For all who are allowing themselves to be led by the Spirit of God are sons of God. For you have not received a spirit of slavery leading again to fear [of God's judgment], but you have received the Spirit of adoption as sons [the Spirit producing sonship], by which we [joyfully] cry, "Abba! Father!"** Romans 8:14-15 (AMP)

The Spirit of the Lord is the Spirit of Sonship. This does not mean adoption in the earthly sense—where adoption implies being brought into a family to which we did not originally belong. Instead, it is a spiritual adoption, a confirmation of maturity in God's family. We have been born again into God's household, and now, God desires to raise us into mature sons who can steward His kingdom.

In Jewish tradition, an heir did not interact directly with the father until an appointed time. Until then, they were under the care of servants and guardians. When the father saw they had matured, he held an adoption ceremony—not to bring them into the family, but to mark their transition into full sonship. From that moment, the heir dealt directly with the father and embraced their household responsibilities.

This is exactly what happens when we receive the Holy Spirit. When the Lord was baptized in the Jordan River, He experienced this moment of adoption:

"And behold a voice from heaven said, 'This is My beloved Son, in whom I am well-pleased and delighted!" Matthew 3:17 (AMP)

From that moment forward, Jesus Christ fully embraced His Father's business. Likewise, when we receive the Holy Spirit, we receive the spirit of adoption—the confirmation of our sonship and the call to take responsibility in the Kingdom.

The hard truth is this: Creation is not waiting for children of God—it is waiting for sons of God.

"For [even the whole] creation (all nature) waits expectantly and longs earnestly for God's sons to be made known [waits for the revealing, the disclosing of their sonship" Romans 8:19 (AMPC)

God's purposes, designs, and plans cannot be accomplished by a Church full of children. There must be sons on earth—mature, refined, and ready to partner with God in His divine agenda. Let us take our rightful place!

Building a Nation of God

The worst mistake is confining ourselves to earthly nationalities. God is raising a divine nation—people of all races, ages, and genders—scattered across the earth as His representatives. *God is building a nation—a people for His own name.* To be part of this, we must mature and align with His purpose, carrying His name, power, and glory. The time to step into our true calling is now.

We must also revisit our mandate. God equips us with grace, and no one is greater—only different in function, empowered by the same Spirit. Every grace is precious in God's sight. No matter what the enemy has done, God restores those who return to Him, realigning them with His purpose. The call to prepare is a call to rediscover and fulfill His plan.

In my years in ministry, I have come to learn and appreciate every grace bestowed on each man as precious in the sight of God. God has never made anything that is of no value. It doesn't matter what the devil has done in your life; that was *merely abuse.* If you come back to God, He will restore you to your *intended purpose,* allowing you to walk in alignment with His divine destiny. The call to prepare is a call to rediscover and fulfill *God's* eternal plan for your life.

As members of this nation we must go beyond *spiritual nationalism,* where our vision is limited to our immediate surroundings. Instead, we must cultivate a desire to *see as God sees,* to look at people and nations through His eyes. If you can pray and fast for your earthly country, then summon that same spirit and intercede for other nations as well.

The worst thing you can do for yourself is identify primarily by your nationality—whether Swazi, Motswana, Mosotho, or South African. "Come out from among them, My people." God is building His own nation, scattered among the nations, a nation where we represent His Kingdom. If you miss this, you'll be consumed by your national identity.

In a vision, someone saw Jesus coming and got excited thinking, "Today, I'll know His nationality." To their amazement, Jesus transformed as he appeared, rotating through faces of various nationalities: Swazi, Mosotho, Motswana, Zimbabwean, South African, Indian, American, Chinese. The person was confused. Let me tell you: Jesus doesn't look like you; we are to look like Him.

Conclusion

In this building time, we must arm ourselves with three critical understandings: who God is, who we are in Him, and what He is doing. Alongside this, we must arm ourselves with humility. If even the slightest trace of pride resides within you, run to the altar and cry out for mercy. Pride has no place in those who are preparing for the weight of His glory. Please be ruthless when dealing with pride, run to God. Do this knowing that you are not running to One who is ready to punish you but to the One who is ready to forgive and help you.

In this season, as we prepare for the revival, we must embrace the humility of Christ. We must adopt the mind of Christ in our lives, allowing His selflessness and obedience to shape our hearts. Without humility, we cannot truly align with the purposes of God for this time.

In the next chapter, we will explore the formation of Christ in man—a transformative process that enables us to carry His presence and fulfil His divine purposes in this end-time revival.

Chapter Eleven
The Formation of Christ

> "*My little children, for whom I am again suffering birth pangs until Christ is completely and permanently formed (molded) within you*"
> **Galatians 4:19 (AMPC)**

One of the greatest issues in the Church today is that many Christians have been entertained, preached to, and even taught—but never built. Teaching alone is not enough. Preaching alone is not enough. Even the Galatian church, having been taught by one of the greatest preachers—Apostle Paul—still found themselves backsliding. This is why Paul, recognizing the root cause, declared that Christ must be formed in them.

Let me tell you this: while both you and I are capable of backsliding, Christ is not. This is why He must be formed in us. When Christ is fully formed, we are no longer reliant on willpower, emotions, or sheer discipline to remain faithful. But, we are transformed from within.

As we discussed in the previous chapter, we have come into a time where God has chosen to build—not merely individuals but a corporate man, a body of believers who will be united as one. This corporate man is the Body of the Lord Jesus Christ.

The Process of Building What Was Lost

God is building in us what we once had. Our fall from our original position was merely a detour in God's divine plan. Now, He is restoring us, forming a new man within us—one that is not just saved but fully aligned with His eternal purpose.

This may sound shocking, but in time, God is incomplete. He is perfect in eternity past and eternity future, but in time, He is not. We were taken out of Him—we are a slice of the divine, as captured by the prophet Isaiah:

> **"Look to the rock from which you were hewn and to the hole in the quarry from which you were dug"**
> *Isaiah 51:1 (AMPC)*

God is building Himself inside us because He is preparing to take us back to the *hole from which we were hewn*. To return, we must be of the *same material* as the rock. If you were to examine a stone and compare it to the mountain from which it was taken, you should see no distinction between the two.

Likewise, when Christ is fully formed in us, we must bear His very nature, so that there is no difference between us and Him. This is important for revival.

This formation of Christ does not happen overnight—it is a process. True transformation is a gradual, intentional process. I often say you can entertain in a short period, but you can not build in a short time. Even a month is too short for this kind of transformation.

We ourselves spent years on the topic of the formation of

Christ—so much so that it remained the central message God gave us. I recall a brother who grew frustrated after a crusade in Botswana because, once again, I preached on the formation of Christ.

During the sermon, I said, "One of you is wondering, 'Why is Simelane still teaching about this?'" Then I answered, "I cannot stop—not until Christ is formed in you." Because that is the goal—until Christ is fully formed, the work is not done.

The same thing happened with Paul and Barnabas, who stayed with the church in Antioch for twelve months. They poured out revelation day and night, shaping the believers until there were real manifestations of Jesus Christ in bodies of clay.

This is what awaits the Church today—not a people who have been taught, but a people who have been built.

When God's building work is complete, the evidence is undeniable—even to those outside the faith. The church in Antioch is proof of this. The transformation in the believers became so evident that even heathens took notice.

They did not need the believers to introduce themselves—instead, the unbelievers coined a new term to describe them:

"Christians."

This label was not originally a title of honor—it was a derogatory remark. It was not the believers who said, "because we follow Christ we will call ourselves Christians", it was the heathens who saw the manifestations of Christ in their lives, and thereafter called them "little Christs" in a derogatory manner. What began as a derogatory label became a testament to their identity in Christ.

This is the evidence of a life that has been built by God—when even the world cannot deny the presence of Christ in you.

Salvation is Only the Beginning

Sadly, religion has made us comfortable that salvation is the end of the story. But when we analyse the scriptures, we come to a different conclusion. The Bible makes it clear:

> **"Who wishes all men to be saved and [increasingly] to perceive and recognize and discern and know precisely and correctly the [divine] Truth"** 1 Timothy 2:4 (AMPC)

Yes, it is true that God wants all men to be saved. But many have placed a full stop where God placed a comma.

There is more.

God not only desires salvation but that we grow—that we recognize, perceive, discern, and come to know the Truth in its fullness. The Word emphasizes "Truth" with a capital "T" because Truth is not merely a concept—it is a Person: Jesus Christ.

Let me repeat this. Salvation is not the final destination but the beginning of a journey. After being saved, a *work of grace* must occur in your life until Christ is fully formed in you.

To illustrate, let's say you plan to walk from Johannesburg to Mbabane. If you take your first step out of Johannesburg, does it mean you have arrived in Mbabane? No!

You still have a journey ahead—a process that requires progress, endurance, and determination. Likewise, salvation is only the first step. If we do not allow this transformative work to unfold, there is no guarantee that we will remain standing when the trumpet sounds.

We must be continually built, continually shaped, continually refined—until Christ is fully formed in us. This is the ultimate plan of heaven for each believer—not just to be saved but to be transformed into the likeness of the Lord Jesus.

Christ in You

To understand the profound difference between those to whom Christ has been taught and those in whom Christ has been formed, one need only compare two distinct churches in the early days of Christianity: the Church of Antioch and the Church of Galatia.

As we have already discussed, the Galatians were preached to by Paul in such a powerful way that he said Christ was graphically portrayed before them during his preaching. Yet, as soon as Paul left, deceivers crept in, and the brethren fell from grace. Expressing his deep frustration, Paul rebuked them:

> **"O you poor and silly and thoughtless and unreflecting and senseless Galatians! Who has fascinated or bewitched or cast a spell over you, unto whom—right before your very eyes—Jesus Christ (the Messiah) was openly and graphically set forth and portrayed as crucified?"** Galatians 3:1 (AMPC)

Meanwhile, the believers in Antioch displayed a striking contrast. Christ had been formed in them. Their faith was not superficial, nor was it dependent on Paul's presence. It was deeply ingrained in their very being. Even in the face of severe persecution and death, they stood firm and unshaken. Christ had been so fully formed in them that denying Him was impossible.

Because the truth is, Christ will never deny Christ.

This is why Paul did not merely preach salvation—he labored for transformation. He declared:

"My little children, for whom I am suffering birth pangs until Christ is completely and permanently formed (molded) within you." Galatians 4:19 (AMP)

What is striking in Paul's statement is the word "again"—implying that this was not his first labor for them.
- The first labor was to bring them into salvation.

- The second labor was to ensure that Christ would be permanently formed in them.

This second labor is crucial. It is not enough for Christ to be merely known or spoken of—He must be formed in us wholly and entirely.

The Mystery of Christ Dwelling in You

Fitting Christ in you is no easy feat. The universe itself cannot contain Him. The heavens are only sufficient to be His throne, and the earth is merely enough to be His footstool. Yet, in His divine wisdom, He has chosen to fit all of Himself within you. This is where the carnal mind struggles. Even the tip of His little finger can fill the whole of you, but that is not what He is doing; He is taking the whole of Himself and filling you with Himself; that is a great mystery.

If you do not think that is a mystery, I challenge you to take a table and try to fit it into a basket. Only then will you begin to grasp the magnitude of the mystery—how the whole of God is being fitted into a man. This mystery is so extraordinary that even the angels cannot fully comprehend it. Yet, it is unfolding in our time and season.

I cannot express how thrilled I am to be alive in this hour. I would not trade this moment for any other in history. This is the most glorious era in the story of the Church—a day when God is building Himself inside man. If this truth weren't found in the Bible, one might dare to call it heresy, but it is the Word of God. Paul himself declared, *"I'm in labor until Christ is formed"* (Galatians 4:19). This is scriptural; we know it is in the Word.

God is forming Himself in you—and He does this through His Word. Let us explore this in scripture so that you do not say it is Simelane saying all manner of things.

> ***"In the beginning [before all time] was the Word [Christ], and the Word was with God, and the Word was God Himself."*** John 1:1 (AMP)

That is why Apostle John can say that we are going to see Him as He is.

> **"Beloved, we are [even here and] now children of God, and it is not yet made clear what we will be [after His coming]. We know that when He comes and is revealed, we will [as His children] be like Him, because we will see Him just as He is [in all His glory]."** 1 John 3:2 (AMP)

But wait! Is the Bible contradicting itself here? The same God who told Moses, *"You cannot see Me and live,"* is now revealing to John that we will see Him in all His Glory and live.

> ***"But, He said, You cannot see My face, for no man shall see Me and live."*** Exodus 33:20 (AMPC)

Is this a contradiction? No! God is not lying. While it is true that it is impossible for man to see God and live, it is perfectly legal for God to see God and live. When Christ is fully formed in you, your identity is so transformed that even angels—who know you by name—will fail to recognize you. Instead, they will see Christ in you. What's more, they will be astonished to see not just one Christ but millions. For all eternity, the angels have only known one Christ, and on that day, they will see countless reflections of Him, an awe-inspiring revelation of God's divine plan.

The Divine Plan of God

This is God's divine plan—you are being built according to His specifications. Salvation is wonderful. Baptism in the Holy Spirit is essential. But heaven has decreed that after salvation, a transformative work of grace must take place in your life until you are exactly as Christ is, so that He may have many brothers.

> *"For those whom He foreknew [of whom He was aware and loved beforehand], He also destined from the beginning [foreordaining them] to be molded into the image of His Son [and share inwardly His likeness], that He might become the firstborn among many brethren."* Romans 8:29 (AMP)

When the Lord Jesus came into this earth, He came as the only begotten Son of God, but it was never the plan of heaven for Him to remain the only one. Heaven's purpose was for Him to be the Firstborn among many. This truth is beautifully illustrated in a statement Jesus Christ made:

> *"I assure you, most solemnly I tell you, Unless a grain of wheat falls into the earth and dies, it remains [just one grain; it never becomes more but lives] by itself alone. But if it dies, it produces many others and yields a rich harvest."* John 12:24 (AMPC)

Though He spoke to an agrarian society, this was not a lesson in agriculture. It was a revelation of a profound spiritual mystery. The Lord was saying I am going to the cross as a Seed from my Father and my Father is going to reap a bumper harvest of sons.

Jesus did not just bring religion; He brought God to earth. Religion says, "Run away from hell," yet it does not equip you with the feet to run. But revelation says, "Have God." We are not trying to escape hell; we have already been delivered from the corruption in the world. What you and I should desire now is for the divine plan to be fulfilled in our lives: And the divine plan is the formation of Christ within us, so that Jesus may be one among many.

The Formation of Christ in Us—A Key to Revival

The formation of Christ in us is absolutely crucial in this time of revival because it is the day of Glory. Only Jesus Christ can carry this glory. In fact, the Bible teaches that He is not only the perfect image of the Father but also the sole expression of the Glory of God. As His Glory is revealed in and through us, the world will witness the fulfillment of this divine plan.

> **"He is the sole expression of the glory of God [the**

Light-being, the out-raying or radiance of the divine], and He is the perfect imprint and very image of [God's] nature, upholding and maintaining and guiding and propelling the universe by His mighty word of power." Hebrews 1:3 (AMPC)

This revival is more than a revelation of God's Glory—it is a confrontation between the forces of good and evil.

As we have mentioned when talking about Eswatini, this revival will drive out demonic powers. It will awaken the Church, shake the foundations of the world, and ignite a battle between light and darkness.

In the next chapter, we will explore why revival is so desperately needed and how it will lead to one of the greatest confrontations in history—advancing the Kingdom of God.

Chapter Twelve

Confrontation Between Right and Wrong

> "**I** have not brought disaster on Israel, but you and your father's household have, by abandoning (rejecting) the commandments of the Lord and by following the Baals."
> *1 Kings 18:18 (AMP)*

Elijah's declaration to King Ahab was as piercing as it was tragic. Standing before the very man he had spent years evading—surviving in the wilderness, fed only by ravens—Elijah exposed the truth: Israel, God's chosen people, had abandoned Him. They had forsaken the true and living God and turned to Baal, a powerless idol. And in doing so, they brought calamity upon themselves.

This was not just a case of ignorance or naivety, but rather of straying. They had seen Him perform mighty wonders—from the plagues in Egypt to the parting of the Red Sea. They had eaten bread from heaven, walked without sickness, and followed His pillar of fire by night. Yet, despite all this, they strayed.

When people who have known God lose their way, the only remedy is revival. Without revival, repentance becomes impossible because sin dulls the heart. It erodes conviction. It numbs the ability to discern right from wrong. While we assume such a departure happens only to those who have never known God, Israel's history proves otherwise. Let us spend some time recounting what the Israelites had seen of God.

A People Who Lived in Daily Miracles

The Israelites' journey from Egypt is one of the greatest demonstrations of God's power and faithfulness. They left Egypt with unshakable certainty in their God. They saw Him humble Pharaoh, split the Red Sea, and destroy their enemies.

> *"there was not one feeble person among their tribes."* Psalm 105:37 (AMPC)

This detail is crucial. Among those who marched out of Egypt were both the young and the old. We gather this from Moses telling Pharaoh that everyone—regardless of age—would leave Egypt (Exodus 10:9). Yet, not a single person was weak or sick. The elderly marched with supernatural strength, undeterred by the desert's harsh conditions or the long journey ahead.

When they rested, it was not out of exhaustion but because the pillar of cloud by day and the pillar of fire by night instructed them to stop. Their movements were dictated solely by God's leading, not by physical limitations.

They were not sustained by their own ability but by the power of God.

- They moved only at God's command—when the pillar of fire by night and the cloud by day signaled them to stop.

- They were fed daily by miracles—manna from heaven and meat that fell like rain.

- They drank from water that flowed from a rock—the very provision of God Himself.

They lived inside a miracle, yet they grew dull in spirit. Jezebel's influence bewitched them. Even those who had once known the truth dined at her table. These were not spiritually ignorant people—they knew the stories of their ancestors' deliverance. They had heard of God's faithfulness. Yet, their hearts turned away.

God had given them steps to ensure that His works were never forgotten:

- He commanded the Israelites to write His laws on their doorposts.

- He instructed them to recount His deeds every morning and evening.

- He built rhythms of remembrance into their daily lives.

Yet, despite all this, their hearts grew dull. Their defection came from a turning of the heart. That is why the Bible warns us to guard the heart, for when it grows dull, even those who have known God can lose their way. The Israelites' story serves as a stark reminder that without vigilance, even a people immersed in God's glory can fail to recognize right from wrong. This is why revival is not just necessary but vital—it reignites the heart and restores the truth.

Yet, even these people—so familiar with the tangible presence and power of God—turned away. This reveals a sobering truth: even those who have experienced the fullness of God's power can stray when their hearts grow dull. *The only cure for a hardened heart is the fire of revival.*

Revival as the Remedy

Revival becomes essential when the hearts of God's people have drifted far from Him. It is not merely a spiritual refreshment but a divine confrontation—a battle between right and wrong, truth and deception, God and Baal. The Israelites' story proves this: revival is not for those who have never known God, but for those who once knew Him and have strayed. Revival rekindles the fire, calls God's people back to Him, and sets the stage for the ultimate confrontation between light and darkness.

A dull heart needs revival. Sin does not just lead people away—it blinds them to their condition. The more they stray, the less they recognize the need for repentance. This is why revival is necessary not just for the lost but also for the Church.

Because God loved Israel, He raised Elijah as an agent of revival. Elijah's mission was not just to stand against false prophets—it was to turn the hearts of the people back to God. In this end-time revival, the same will be required. The coming revival will not be comfortable—it will be marked by confrontations between good and evil, righteousness and wickedness. Just as Mount Carmel became a battleground for truth, this revival will expose and uproot what is false.

Elijah, an Agent for Revival

Elijah's confrontation on Mount Carmel was not merely a battle of opposing forces; it was about reclaiming the heart of a nation. He rebuked the Israelites for abandoning the commandments of the Lord and succumbing to idolatry. They had turned so far from God that they were eating at Jezebel's table, participating in her false worship. Their spiritual dullness was so severe that Elijah had to draw a clear line, saying:

> **"How long will you hesitate between two opinions? If the Lord is God, follow Him; but if Baal, follow him."** 1 Kings 18:21 (AMP)

Elijah's words pierced through their spiritual coldness, exposing their indecision and the depths of their departure from God. The revival on Mount Carmel was not just about fire falling from heaven; it was about the fire of conviction igniting their hearts once more.

The greatest tragedy of falling away is the dullness of the heart that follows. What was once known as sin becomes acceptable—even justified. Israel had reached this level of spiritual numbness.

When Elijah stood on Mount Carmel, he exposed their indecision when asking who they would follow.

Dead silence. Imagine this! These were God's chosen people. They had seen His wonders. Yet, when faced with the question of who they would serve, they could not respond.

It was only after God sent fire from heaven that they fell on their faces and cried:

> **"The Lord, He is God! The Lord, He is God!"** 1 Kings 18:39 (AMP)

This was a revival—a nation turning back to the true and living God in a single moment. These words from the Israelites came after God demonstrated His power on Mount Carmel, vindicating Elijah's stand for righteousness. This was not just a victory for Elijah—it was a large-scale revival. Standing alone against 450 prophets of Baal and 400 prophets of Asherah, Elijah became the vessel through which God revealed Himself to His people.

The story of Elijah on Mount Carmel reveals key truths about revival. It shows the dangers of sin, the courage needed to stand for God, and the inevitable battle between truth and deception. These are some of the topics I want us to explore below.

1. **Sin is Dangerous and Has Consequences:** It leads people away from God and into destruction, as seen when Israel's idolatry brought drought and suffering, proving that false gods will always fail.

2. **Revival Requires Taking a Stand—But You Are Never Alone:** Elijah stood for God even when it seemed he was alone, yet God always preserves a faithful remnant and strengthens those who stand for truth.

3. **Revival is a Confrontation Between Good and Evil:** It is a battle between truth and deception, but God's power always prevails, demanding boldness, faith, and commitment from His people.

Sin is Dangerous

Exactly as the title says—sin is dangerous. A lot of preachers have fallen into this trap.

I have said this before, and I will say it again: in revival, we must be ruthless with sin. I will emphasize this as much as possible because I want you to succeed. More importantly, God wants you to succeed.

Perhaps you're wondering:

- **How could the Israelites have fallen so far?**

- How could they—descendants of Abraham, Isaac, and Jacob—be unsure of who to worship?

Sin dulls the spirit.

Sin dulls conviction, weakens discernment, and makes the heart insensitive to God's voice. When a heart is hardened, even the most powerful sermon will fall on deaf ears. This is why revival is not about entertainment—it is about the fire of conviction igniting the hearts of God's people once again.

When Elijah stood before them, calling them to repentance, their spiritual ears were closed. Israelites had grown so spiritually dull that they no longer recognized God, nor could they respond to the call of His servants. In today's terms, we might say that Elijah's powerful sermon, calling them to repentance, fell on deaf ears. Tragically, this is not unique to the Israelites. Even today, people made by God reject the Word delivered by His messengers.

This spiritual dullness does more than make people resistant—it blinds them to the authority of God's chosen servants. When Elijah called out to them, asking, "For how long will you people waver between two opinions?" no one repented. The sadness here is that Israel, the chosen nation, failed to recognize what even a non-Israelite had discerned.

Think about it! These were the same people whose ancestors had seen the Red Sea part, eaten bread from heaven, walked without sickness, and been led by God Himself—yet they could not even answer a simple question about who they would serve.

The issue with sin is that people will often try to justify it. We can only imagine what the Israelites might have said during Elijah's call to repentance. Perhaps they justified their allegiance to Jezebel, saying, *But Jezebel speaks so eloquently. She's kind to us. She feeds us.* The Bible confirms their dependency on her provision, noting that "they ate at

Jezebel's table" (I Kings 18:19). What's more shocking is the caliber of people eating there. Some had once been prophets of Jehovah, yet now they sat at Jezebel's table, blessing their food in the name of Baal instead of the Lord's.

This highlights the devastating impact of spiritual dullness. These were not strangers to God—they had been His prophets, His people. But sin and compromise had blunted their spirits to the point where they no longer recognized the God who had brought them out of Egypt, nor could they hear His call to repentance. Sin is not just a bad habit—it is a force that dulls the spirit. It is a slow numbing until you can no longer see, hear, or even desire God.

This is why I keep saying: Be ruthless with sin.

That is why I have repeatedly emphasized the need for self-examination, even for pastors and leaders. Sin must be confronted ruthlessly before it leads to compromise. In its truest form, revival is the only remedy for such a state. It breaks through spiritual numbness, shatters deception, and reignites the truth in the hearts of God's people.

Never Alone

This revival sets the precedent for what is to come in our time. Elijah stood against 450 prophets of Baal and 400 prophets of Asherah—yet he was not intimidated.

> **"I alone remain a prophet of the Lord, while Baal's prophets are 450 men. Now let them give us two oxen... Then you call on the name of your god, and I will call on the name of the Lord; and the god who answers by fire, He is God."** 1 Kings 18:22-24 (AMP)

There will be moments in this end-time revival where you will have to stand alone.

- Not everyone will believe the message.

- Not everyone will celebrate what God is doing.

- Not everyone will have the courage to stand.

But God is raising men and women who will stand anyway—just as Elijah did. In our early days at Madlangempisi, we saw this firsthand. We had confrontations with those sent from the enemy's camp. But every time, God's power prevailed. There will be battles in this revival, but there will also be victories. No matter how alone Elijah felt, God was always there with him.

On the run from Ahab and famished, Elijah was commanded by God to go to a widow in Zarephath. Without hesitation or question, the widow recognized Elijah as a prophet of God and obeyed. Israel, on the other hand, could not see or acknowledge the God of their fathers. Many years later, even the Lord Jesus would recall the obedience of this widow:

> **"But in truth I say to you, there were many widows in Israel in the days of Elijah, when the sky was closed up for three years and six months, when a great famine came over all the land; and yet Elijah was not sent [by the Lord] to a single one of them, but only to Zarephath in the land of Sidon, to a woman who was a widow."** Luke 4:25–26 (AMP)

For her obedience, God provided for her supernaturally. When Elijah arrived, she had just enough oil for one meal. But with the presence of the prophet and her act of faith, the oil and flour miraculously sustained her household for years. Yet, while this foreign widow recognized and welcomed the prophet, Israel remained blind to God's hand in their lives.

In revival, God will always be with you. He will bring the right people to stand with you, to labor alongside you—but your role is to be in position and take a stand.

Elijah stood boldly on Mount Carmel, seemingly alone against hundreds of false prophets. Yet he was never truly alone. God was with him, and God had preserved others who had not bowed to Baal.

In the same way, when you step into the work of revival, you may feel isolated at times, but heaven backs you. God will send those who are called to labor with you. Your responsibility is to be where He has placed you and refuse to waver.

Confrontation

The battleground was set. There had to be a confrontation between good and evil, between truth and deception. Even in this day and age, God has assured us there will be another confrontation. It's crucial to understand that just because God is moving in revival does not mean the devil will retreat passively. When God declares the end from the beginning, He is essentially challenging the enemy: "Try and see if you can stop it." God does not promise that His work will proceed because the devil is absent. Rather, He promises to act in the full view of the enemy, unfazed by his schemes. Through the Prophet Isaiah, we are reminded of this promise:

> **"So shall they fear the name of the LORD from the west, and his glory from the rising of the sun. When the enemy shall come in like a flood, the Spirit of the LORD shall lift up a standard against him."** Isaiah 59:19 (KJV)

With unwavering faith, Elijah stood boldly before a nation that had lost its way. The Bible does not record if Elijah was an eloquent speaker, but one thing is clear: he had an audience with God. The children of Israel were too far gone in their spiritual dullness to be moved by eloquence or even a powerful sermon. When Elijah confronted their divided worship of Baal and God, they did not respond with repentance.

- For some, turning from false worship was difficult—not because they believed in Baal, but because their livelihood depended on Jezebel.

- It is often tough for some people to turn from the source of their living, even when it is in conflict with God.

But we must remember, He is a jealous God.

The confrontation began. We are familiar with the story. Elijah challenged the prophets of Baal to a test: let their god prove himself by bringing fire from heaven. But when their idol failed, Elijah, confident in his God, began to mock them: "Maybe your god is a statue. Perhaps he's asleep. Shout louder; he might be far away." Yet, their idol remained powerless.

However, Your God is all powerful. In revival time, we will challenge the power of the so called idols of the nations. Revival is not just a spiritual awakening; it is a divine confrontation. It exposes the emptiness of false idols and reestablishes the authority of God over the hearts of His people.

With the prophets of Baal humiliated and powerless, what followed was a profound lesson in faith and trust. Elijah didn't merely ask God to prove Himself; he intentionally made the challenge seem insurmountable.

- He ordered water to be poured over the altar, saturating the wood and filling a trench around it, ensuring no one could claim the fire came from hidden embers or natural causes.

- To the bystander, it might have seemed as though Elijah was making it harder for himself.

- But in truth, he was magnifying the power of God, ensuring that His miracle would be undeniable.

Then, with one prayer, Elijah called upon the Lord—and heaven responded. Fire descended, consuming the sacrifice, the wood, the stones, even the water in the trench. The people could no longer deny it. Overwhelmed, they fell on their faces, crying out: "The Lord, He is God! The Lord, He is God!"

In that moment, the nation of Israel turned back to their God, saved and redeemed in a single day. The revival at Mount Carmel was not just a moment in history—it was a foreshadowing of a global outpouring to come. In the next chapter, we will explore how God will move again, this time sweeping across entire continents with the same undeniable power.

Chapter Thirteen

A Continent Can Be Saved in One Day

"Who has heard of such a thing? Who has seen such things? Can a land be born in one day? Or can a nation be brought forth in a moment? As soon as Zion was in labor, she also brought forth her sons."
Isaiah 66:8 (AMP)

When revival comes, it brings results that are explosive and undeniable. The battle between light and darkness intensifies, setting the stage for breakthroughs unlike anything the world has ever seen.

I remember when God spoke to us during one of our conferences:

"You are going to witness breakthrough after breakthrough, victory after victory."

At the time, we rejoiced in this promise, unaware of the deeper reality embedded within it. Every breakthrough, every victory, would come through battle. And the size of the battle would determine the magnitude of the victory.

When heaven draws near, angelic activity increases dramatically.

The devil, though limited in understanding, senses the shift. He perceives that something is about to happen in the spiritual realm. Even without knowing the details, he moves to disrupt it.

Consider the events surrounding the birth of Moses:

- The enemy sensed that deliverance was at hand but did not know how or through whom it would come.

- In response, he issued a decree to kill all male children.

- Yet, despite every effort to thwart God's plan, deliverance still came.

The same pattern repeated with the birth of Jesus. The enemy, sensing a great move of God, once again attempted mass slaughter to prevent it. The exact same blueprint.

And now, in our time, a similar thing is happening. The enemy knows something is coming. He anticipates revival, but he cannot pinpoint its source or stop the will of God. He does not know who will obey and usher in this move of the Spirit. All he sees is the increased angelic activity upon the earth.

We stand on the brink of the greatest revival in history—an unprecedented move of God. Revival is at hand. Though the enemy will try to hinder it, he will ultimately fail.

I have often said that when the devil sees the real thing coming, he releases a counterfeit. He attempts to exhaust people with distractions, deceptions, and false revivals so that by the time the genuine move of God arrives, people are weary.

But we must hold on. Revival is coming.

A Nation Saved in One Day

Reading all of this, you may think, *The time is too short for all God has promised to come to pass.*

You might wonder, *When will these things happen?*

But let me tell you: God can do one thing in Africa, and the entire continent will turn to Him.

He can do the same in Europe, in Australia, in the Americas, and beyond.

In 1984, when God told me that millions would be saved in a single day, I struggled to comprehend it. Coming from Eswatini, a nation of only one million people, it seemed impossible. But now, as we witness the raindrops of revival, we see that we are in the day of fulfillment.

Continents will be saved in a single day. And you may ask, *How is that possible?*

It may sound like too much—like I am dreaming. But when God, who exists outside of time, steps in, there are no limits. He can accomplish in an instant what would otherwise take generations.

We have already seen glimpses of this in Scripture we have covered in this book:

- **Samaria:** A whole city turned to God in a moment because of the obedience of one woman and the obedience of Jesus.

- **Mount Carmel:** A whole nation turned back to God in an instant because of Elijah's obedience.

But in our time, we will witness something even greater—entire nations and continents being born again in a single day.

> **"So will My word be which goes out of My mouth; It will not return to Me void (useless, without result), Without accomplishing what I desire, And without succeeding in the matter for which I sent it."** Isaiah 55:11 (AMP)

Our part in this is simple yet profound: believe everything God has spoken and expect Him to move on the earth.

We must be ready to obey, just as the Lord Jesus obeyed and brought revival to Samaria, and just as Elijah obeyed and turned Israel back to God. We stand firmly on His word, knowing that it will not return void. People already know that God speaks. If you grew up in Eswatini or as part of our community, you know this well. He spoke before the airport was built. He spoke about gold hidden in the mountains, and it was later discovered.

And as He continues to speak and rend the heavens, people will not just acknowledge that God speaks—they will cry out:

"He alone is God! He alone is God!"

How Will It Happen?

Now to answer this question for those who may be asking themselves. It will happen through two things:

1. Intimate knowledge of God

2. The power that comes from the presence of God

Let us explore these subtopics further below.

1. Victory Through Intimate Knowledge of God

As we discussed in the previous chapter, Elijah's confidence came from his intimate knowledge of God. He knew his God. That is why, even when the odds were against him, he stood firm.

In fact, he deliberately made the situation appear even more impossible by drenching the altar with water before calling on God. And when he prayed, fire fell. There was no doubt.

"But the people who do know their God shall be strong, and do exploits." Daniel 11:32 (KJV)

That same God is moving again in our time. Just as He delivered Israel in a single day, He will deliver entire nations and continents in a single day during this coming revival. He will use bold people who know Him.

2. Victory Through Demonstration of the Power of God

As we discussed in the vision of the powerless church, everything changes when power comes down. The Israelites were not changed by a well-crafted sermon. We don't read about Elijah's eloquence or persuasive ability. They were changed because the power of God came down. An entire nation fell to the ground and acknowledged God's Lordship.

This was not a moment of mere conviction or emotion. This was a true revival. A total turning back to God—not by human reasoning, but by the manifest presence of the Almighty. When God rends the heavens, His power is undeniable. His mighty works cause nations to bow before Him.

And when this power comes, it transforms even the hardest heart. It strengthens even the weakest believer. It leaves no room for compromise. In the Welsh Revival, football stadiums, once filled with passionate fans, were emptied as people abandoned everything to seek God.

But in our time, we will not abandon the stadiums.

We will fill them!

I have seen it. God showed me stadiums overflowing with people during the revival.

And when the fire of God falls, just as on Mount Carmel, no one will hesitate. They will cry out in conviction: "He is Lord! He is God!" They will turn 180 degrees, forsaking false gods and clinging to Jehovah. This will not be a momentary experience—this will be transformation.

As we close this chapter, let us hold on to this truth: *everything God has spoken will come to pass.* His Word is true, and He will fulfill it. In the next chapter, we will delve deeper into God's promises for one of the world's continents in this extraordinary time of revival.

Chapter Fourteen

Good Morning Africa

> "Instead of your shame you will receive a double portion, and instead of disgrace you will rejoice in your inheritance; and so you will inherit a double portion in your land, and everlasting joy will be yours."
> **Isaiah 61:7 (NIV)**

"Good morning, Africa." These are the words I heard. *"Good morning, Africa."* The Lord declared a new dawn for the continent

It is no secret that throughout history, Africa has faced ridicule and dejection. Many have mocked Africa, questioning the fervent prayers of its people, given the poverty that has long plagued the land. They have wondered why God remains silent while Africans suffer. But as a prophet of God, I stand here today to declare that God has remembered Africa. He is writing a new story for the continent.

Historically, God has spoken to the world from every continent but Africa. But it has pleased the Father, in this season, to stand in Africa and speak. He has chosen Africa not only as a recipient of His Word but also as a platform from which He will declare His purposes to the nations.

You may be wondering, "Does this contradict what Simelane mentioned earlier in this book?" The answer is no. The revival that God is orchestrating will not be confined to one country or continent—it is a global revival. Yet, God has revealed that He has specific and significant plans for Africa. As we prepare for this mighty move, we must take note of what He is doing on this continent.

Hope for Africa

God has revealed that revival will first break out in Africa, and then spread to the rest of the world. In the vision we shared earlier, Africa was covered in black soot, and the mighty wind blew the soot away, revealing the magnificent beauty beneath. This vision is a powerful symbol of what revival will do for Africa: it will transform the continent into a beacon of hope and a symbol of God's glory.

God has affirmed that when revival breaks out, it will usher in unprecedented economic advancement for Africa. As His presence descends heavily and His mighty hand moves, human understanding will be opened in ways we never imagined. New insights and innovations will emerge, propelling the continent forward and transforming it into a leader in innovation. Shockingly to many, Africa will soon catch up with the rest of the world in terms of technological and economic decision-making.

These advancements will serve the revival, making communication and transportation easier, and improving the welfare of people across Africa and beyond. When God first spoke to us about this, Africa was far behind in these areas. But today, we can already see the beginning of this transformation. From groundbreaking innovations in medical science to thriving startups reaching billion-dollar valuations, the winds of change are evident. Something remarkable is happening in Africa.

God has also spoken specifically about several countries on the continent and the things He will do for them. One example that stands out is my home country of Eswatini. In addition to the fulfilled prophecy regarding the new international airport capable of handling large jets, God showed me a vision of multitudes bringing their sick—even their dead—to Eswatini for divine help. People came from distant continents, saying, "Let us take them to Eswatini, for that is where help can be found." The crowds were overwhelming—so much so that the influx of people was larger than Eswatini's entire population.

This foretold influx underscores how economic development will facilitate revival, making it both efficient and impactful. Infrastructure development, innovation, and God's divine hand will ensure that Africa plays a leading role in this global awakening.

Another example I was recently reminded of happened while we were preaching in Mozambique. God told us there would be a bridge over the ocean. At the time, it didn't make much sense. But when God speaks, our role isn't to understand—it's simply to *say* what He says. So, we declared it.

Years later someone reminded me of that word during a conversation about God's faithfulness. They said, "That bridge now exists in Maputo." And it does.

Completed in 2018, the Maputo-Katembe Bridge stretches across Maputo Bay and it is now recognized as the longest suspension bridge in Africa. The award winning bridge has drastically reduced travel time between Mozambique and South Africa, and is facilitating major economic development in the region.

Preparation for revival is well on the way.

As much as this revival is for all nations, God has declared that Africa will rise. It will lead in innovation and spiritual renewal, and the revival will spread mightily from there.

Preparing Africa for the World

The plan of God concerning Africa includes the operation of the gifts of the Holy Spirit in an unprecedented way. While other nations once brought the Gospel to Africa, Africans will now carry the Gospel of power to the nations. This is a crucial part of God's redemptive plan for the continent.

We are already beginning to see this shift take place. Many Africans who left for work or study in the West are now starting churches and opening branches there. This is a powerful sign of what is to come. However, it is often heartbreaking to witness the state of some of the countries that once sent missionaries to Africa. In many Western nations, churches are closing at alarming rates. Some buildings are being sold off and repurposed into bars, concert venues, tourist attraction areas or other secular spaces.

Yet, in the midst of this, Africa is rising as a beacon of faith. It will carry the gospel to the ends of the earth, fulfilling the words of the Lord Jesus:

> *"This good news of the kingdom [the gospel] will be preached throughout the whole world as a testimony to all the nations, and then the end [of the age] will come."* Matthew 24:14 (AMP)

It is crucial to recognize that the gospel that Africa will carry is a gospel of power—a gospel that is accompanied by signs, wonders, and miracles. The gospel Jesus Christ spoke of is not one of empty words or mere noise. It is not a gospel that simply fills the air with sound but one that carries the authority of God. The power of the gospel is not only to be preached but demonstrated. Unfortunately, in some places, people have heard about the gospel but found only noise, without the manifestation of the power and presence of God.

The gospel that will emerge from Africa will be one of transformation—a gospel that is alive with the power of God. We will carry that power because we are one with the God of signs and wonders. We are one with the God of miracles. For Africa to fully fulfill this mission, Christ must be formed in His people.

During a powerful meeting in Zimbabwe, the Lord spoke to us, declaring that He would reveal the nature of Christ in Africa. During that meeting, one of our brethren had a vision: a rock fell from above and shattered into countless pieces. As the rock broke apart, the fragments entered the Christians in Africa. God revealed that this vision symbolized the unveiling of Christ across the continent.

The world is waiting. The world is ready for what God has deposited in Africa. The revelation that God is downloading in different parts of the continent is something other nations are longing for.

Out of Africa, there is rising a Divine Sound—not a voice of mere eloquence but a Voice that carries the weight of God. It is a Word that transforms, a Word that carries the power to shift nations and align hearts with the purposes of heaven. This sound will not be a mere message; it will be a manifestation of the power of God.

Africa, the stage is set. God is revealing Christ in us, and through this, the world will witness the Glory of God in a way it has never seen before.

The dawn of this new season has arrived, and with it comes the power and Glory of God. It is time for Africa to rise and take its place in the fulfillment of God's redemptive plan for the nations.

"Good morning Africa," says the LORD.

Chapter Fifteen

Every Word of God Will Come to Fulfilment

"Then said the Lord to me, You have seen well, for I am alert and active, watching over My word to perform it."
Jeremiah 1:12 (AMPC)

The things God has spoken so far may seem like a tall order—even to me, someone who has heard Him speak them firsthand. Yet, I have learned to trust Him completely. In this chapter, I aim to encourage you to lean fully on His Word, for it is truly our only choice.

The Bible presents lessons for our journey, reminding us to trust in the One who fulfills every Word He speaks. In recent chapters, we have drawn lessons from the life of Elijah, who shows us that no matter how anointed we are, we will encounter suffering. These sufferings, however, are not meant to break us but to propel us to the next level of glory.

"Was it not necessary for the Christ to suffer these

things and [only then to] enter His glory?" Luke 24:26 (AMP)

Through these trials, we must hold onto the truth that our God will bring to fulfillment every word He has spoken. The one who gives the Word is faithful to fulfill it. As we prepare for the greatest revival, we must trust Him wholeheartedly, especially as He does things that we—and the world—have never seen before.

Hold On to His Word

Elijah's journey provides a profound example of trusting God. After declaring a prophecy of drought, Elijah had to go into hiding under God's instruction (I Kings 17:1-2). Imagine the weight of such a prophecy: declaring that there would be no rain, knowing how critical water was to the survival of the people. The prophet had to live under the prophecy. This was not a private declaration—it was public, and everyone knew who had spoken it.

With the prophecy came a cost, not only to the people but also to Elijah himself. God told him to hide, not because God could not protect him in other ways, but because obedience to God's Word is often the vehicle of His protection. When God says go in hiding, it would be foolish of you to turn around and say "but God you are so big, what about your angels?" As the pandemic taught us, do not be guilty of presumption.

Ahab and his men scoured Israel and even neighboring countries, searching for Elijah. Yet, they could not find him because he was obediently hiding where God had instructed. This demonstrates a vital lesson: when God gives an instruction and you follow it, you are under His protection.

Later, the same God who told Elijah to hide issued a new instruction: "Go, show yourself to Ahab" (1 Kings 18:1). Imagine being Elijah at that moment—the God who told him to avoid danger was now sending him directly into the lion's den. But Elijah obeyed, trusting that the God who fulfilled His word by stopping the rain would now fulfill His word by sending it again.

Elijah's story highlights the importance of obedience and trust in God's Word. As we step into this season of revival, we, too, are called to trust in His promises, even when they seem daunting. God is alert and active, watching over His word to perform it (Jeremiah 1:12).

At this point, God could have chosen any means to deliver His message. He could have assigned angels if He willed. Yet, He turned His Word towards Elijah and called him to show himself to Ahab. This is a profound reminder for us: our comfort and security, even in this revival, will come because we are in His will.

I often remind members of our church that just because God will be moving mightily in revival does not mean the devil will fold his arms and watch. The enemy will be active, but our boldness comes from knowing that we stand in alignment with God's will.

When Elijah received the instruction to reveal himself, it went against all human logic. Imagine revealing yourself to the very people who had searched high and low for you, with a death warrant looming over your head. Even Obadiah, a faithful servant of God who had hidden and fed a hundred prophets from Jezebel, was alarmed by Elijah's boldness.

> **"But he said, "What sin have I committed, that you would hand over your servant to Ahab to put me to death? As the Lord your God lives, there is no nation or kingdom where my master has not sent messengers to seek you; and when they said, 'He is not here,' Ahab made the kingdom or nation swear that they**

> **had not found you. And now you are saying, 'Go, tell your master, "Behold, Elijah [is here]."' And as soon as I leave you, the Spirit of the Lord will carry you to a place I do not know; so when I come to tell Ahab and he does not find you, he will kill me. Yet your servant has [reverently] feared the Lord from my youth."** 1 Kings 18: 9-12 (AMP)

Elijah's boldness was rooted in his unwavering trust in God. He reassured Obadiah, "Go and tell Ahab, I'm not going away; when he comes, he will find me here" (1 Kings 18:15). Elijah's courage came from the knowledge that the God who gave him the Word would also fulfill it. This courage is anchored in knowing that we are not prophesying our own wishes but declaring the Word of God. If you speak your own words, you must fulfill them; but if you speak God's Word, He will fulfill it.

The Faithfulness of God to Fulfill His Word

God's faithfulness to His Word is evident throughout history. When He called Moses, a man who could barely speak, to be His spokesperson before Pharaoh, it was not about Moses' abilities but about the God he carried. God showed that it does not matter what you lack; what matters is who you carry. When it comes to His plans, God can open any mouth and use any vessel at the appointed time.

God has spoken to us with clarity: the revival is here. The raindrops of revival are already falling, and He is fulfilling His Word. We see His faithfulness even in how He called Moses, a man who struggled to speak, to be His spokesperson before Pharaoh. Moses's limitations didn't matter; what mattered was that he carried the Word of God. If you carry God, even your perceived inadequacies become irrelevant, because He equips those He calls. Similarly, God has consistently used people who felt unqualified or unworthy in the natural.

Take Oral Roberts as an example. Despite his initial limitations, God used him in remarkable ways. Personally, I can testify to this truth. I, too, was a stammerer, but when God called me, He removed that limitation. The One who made your mouth can open it at the right time. Your weaknesses do not disqualify you from fulfilling God's purposes; rather, they set the stage for His glory to shine through you.

A revival once swept through a region in America, ignited by a man known for his severe stutter. When God called him, he was perplexed: "How can God use me when I can't speak a sentence without stuttering?" He had struggled throughout his life, often reduced to tears when mocked by classmates for his speech impediment.

Seeking counsel, he confided in a friend, saying, "There's nothing I can do. How can God call me?" His friend replied, "I know one thing you can do—you can pray." Embracing this, the man dedicated himself to a life of prayer.

One day, as he was on his way to pray, he encountered a large group of people heading to perform their customary rituals. Filled with holy passion, he felt compelled to address them. Despite not knowing their language and his inability to speak fluently, he stepped forward. Miraculously, God enabled him to speak clearly. Among the crowd was a man under the influence of alcohol who, remarkably, served as his interpreter.

He delivered a powerful sermon, and the entire crowd was moved. They turned away from their previous path and embraced the message he shared. A revival broke out because one man, despite his perceived limitations, chose to carry God within him.

The examples above are just a glimpse of how God fulfills His Word and uses people who might not be the first choice in the eyes of man. I hope these stories have stirred your faith. When preaching, I often say:

Simelane's definition of faith is simply taking it that God is telling the truth. When God speaks, He fulfills His Word. When He calls you to something, trust Him fully.

Believe God

God has given us a lot of prophecies—some simple and others requiring great faith. One day, God gave us a prophecy in the presence of a man who was not mentally stable. This man heard the prophecy as clearly as the rest of us. God was speaking about a river—a riverbed, to be exact. At the time, there was no water flowing in it, only the dry, empty bed remained. But God gave us a word, and we prophesied to that river, declaring that water would flow there again.

In time, God fulfilled His Word. One day, as I passed by that place, water was indeed flowing in the riverbed. The same man who had been there when the prophecy was given was with us, that day. I said to him, "Hey, look, water is flowing here!" To which the man, in his simple and unwavering faith, replied, "We are not surprised because we heard God say the water would flow."

That moment has stayed with me, a reminder of God's faithfulness to fulfill His Word. Even a man deemed unstable by the world could believe God's prophecy without hesitation, and that is the kind of faith God calls us to have. When God speaks, it is as good as done. His Word never returns void.

Now that your faith has been strengthened, we are ready to move into the next chapter, where we will delve into the supernatural—one of the major themes of this end-time revival.

Chapter Sixteen

Season of the Supernatural

"God is spirit [the Source of life, yet invisible to mankind], and those who worship Him must worship in spirit and truth."
John 4:24 (AMP)

The collision of the heavens with the earth always results in supernatural experiences. The supernatural, by definition, refers to occurrences, manifestations, or experiences that go beyond the natural laws of the physical world and point directly to divine or spiritual intervention. In such a time, our role is not just to witness the miraculous, but to expect the unexpected, for God often moves in ways beyond our comprehension.

One of the defining marks of this revival will be supernatural translations—people being transported from one place to another by a spiritual mode of transport rather than the conventional forms we know.

God is Spirit

To understand this, we must first recognize that our God is Spirit, and we too are spiritual beings. Although we live in a physical body, our true essence is spirit. It often happens that at times people will leave their countries and immigrate to other countries for a short time, they get a two months visa or a six months visa. However, people will at times extend their stay and end up staying for a year or two or even for the rest of their lives in the place. Much like a traveler who moves to a new country and stays so long that they begin to think of it as home, we too have dwelt in the physical body for so long that many believe it is our permanent residence. However, the truth is that we are spirit beings temporarily housed in a physical body.

Our big Brother, the Lord Jesus, exemplified this understanding. After preaching and performing works, the Bible often notes that He would withdraw to pray and commune with the Father, returning to the Spirit. He lived fully aware of His spiritual nature and His connection to the Father, and God is calling us to do the same. He desires us to go beyond salvation and experience the world of the Spirit.

This concept is critical in the time we have come to, as God has promised that supernatural translations will be a hallmark of this revival. It is, therefore, essential that we align ourselves with the Spirit to operate in this dimension. We ourselves should be in the Spirit. Consider the experience of Apostle John on the island of Patmos. He describes how, at the words "Come up hither," he was immediately dislodged from his physical body into the Spirit and encountered the divine:

> *"After this I looked, and, behold, a door was opened in heaven: and the first voice which I had heard was as it were of a trumpet talking with me; which said,*

> *Come up hither, and I will shew thee things which must be hereafter. And immediately I was in the spirit: and, behold, a throne was set in heaven, and one sat on the throne."* Revelation 4:1-2 (KJV)

We all must open our ears to hear the words "Come up hither," because we are being called to live in the Spirit by our Lord Jesus Christ. The example of John is wonderful news for us, as he was human just like you and me. This means that even in this time that God has brought us to, we too can experience supernatural translations and live in the Spirit. Instances of the supernatural are woven throughout the Bible. When speaking to Nathaniel, the Lord Jesus assured him that he would witness the supernatural in his day:

> *"Then He said to him, I assure you, most solemnly I tell you all, you shall see heaven opened, and the angels of God ascending and descending upon the Son of Man!"* John 1:51 (AMPC)

I mention such stories to tease in you a desire for the supernatural. Both John and Nathaniel were human, yet they had access to the world of the spirit. These are not fairy tales or far-fetched ideas. They are testimonies of what God has done before and what He will do again. And now, in the season of the supernatural, God has declared that these manifestations will happen even more frequently.

It is not because we are special or more deserving, but because we have entered a divine season where this must happen as part of God fulfilling His Word. Every unique experience in this revival is a testament to God's faithfulness, not our worthiness. His purpose for this time requires that the supernatural becomes a regular reality. Let us, therefore, prepare ourselves to embrace this dimension and hunger for all that God has promised.

Examples of Translations

Translations are not random; they serve the purposes of God, whether to deliver a message, bring the Gospel to new territories, or prophesy His plans for His people. They reveal the boundless power of God and underscore the importance of obedience and alignment with His will. In this revival season, translations will become a significant hallmark of how God moves among His people.

God first spoke to me about translations in 1984. Since then, I have witnessed and learned about the many translations that have taken place throughout history. These are not new occurrences; they have been a notable feature of the supernatural in ministry. For example, translations were a remarkable part of John G. Lake's ministry. However, as with all moves of God, translations are deeply rooted in submitting to His leading.

One time, while we were preaching in Piggs Peak, Eswatini, God instructed us to pray for a specific lady at exactly 7 PM. As we have discussed in prior chapters, accurate and prompt obedience is critical in the things of God. We shared the instruction with her, emphasizing the need to prepare for a spiritual journey. When the clock struck 7 PM, we prayed for her, and God took her into the spirit. She returned 12 hours later, in the morning, and her testimony left us in awe. She recounted how she had gone to many places across continents, preaching and prophesying the Word of God. She was even taken to boats, where she delivered messages from the Lord, strengthening people's faith through prophecy.

This experience illustrates the possibilities that exist because we are both body and spirit. In translations, what is "transported" can vary. Sometimes, it may only be the spirit that is translated. Other times, both the body and spirit are transported. A biblical example of this is found in Acts 8, where the Spirit of God commanded Philip to leave Samaria and go to a desert. Philip's body and spirit were translated, not by human means, but by divine intervention. This translation had a purpose: to meet the Ethiopian eunuch and share the Gospel. Philip didn't walk there; he was supernaturally transported by the Spirit of God.

This extraordinary event is a powerful reminder of the importance of knowing God's voice well. Imagine how challenging it must have been for Philip to leave a massive revival in Samaria to attend to one person in a desert. Yet, because he knew the voice of God, he obeyed without hesitation. This goes back to dealing with our hearts. Imagine if his heart stood in the way of obedience.

It is essential for us, too, to become so attuned to God's voice that when He speaks, we simply go. Philip's obedience shows that God's assignments are not always about numbers but about His divine purpose. The result of this seemingly singular mission was that the eunuch encountered the Gospel, rejoiced, and likely became a vessel to spread the Good News further.

The Bible goes on to detail that after this encounter, Philip experienced yet another translation. After baptizing the eunuch, the Spirit of the Lord carried him to another town to preach the Gospel. He was moved supernaturally from place to place, spreading the message of salvation.

> *"And when they came up out of the water, the Spirit of the Lord [suddenly] caught away Philip; and the eunuch saw him no more, and he went on his way rejoicing. But Philip was found at Azotus, and passing on he preached the good news (Gospel) to all the towns until he reached Caesarea."* Acts 8:39-40

(AMPC)

Another example of a supernatural translation in the Bible is with Elijah. In the conversation between Elijah and Obadiah, we gain insight into how Elijah was known for being translated by the Spirit of the Lord. Some instances of his translations may not have been written down explicitly, but this dialogue gives us a glimpse into how commonly it was associated with him.

After Elijah returned from hiding, he instructed Obadiah to go and tell King Ahab that he was there. Obadiah's reaction reveals much about Elijah's supernatural experiences. In 1 Kings 18:11-12 (AMP), Obadiah responds:

> **"And now you are saying, 'Go tell your master, "Behold, Elijah is here"'. And as soon as I leave you, the Spirit of the Lord will carry you to a place I do not know; so when I come and tell Ahab and he does not find you, he will kill me…"**

This conversation highlights that even Obadiah understood Elijah's reputation for being supernaturally translated by the Spirit of the Lord to unknown locations. This wasn't just a rumor; it was a known aspect of Elijah's walk with God.

These are the kind of supernatural translations we can expect to see in our time. Just as it was a defining mark of Elijah's ministry, God is preparing to demonstrate this same level of supernatural movement in the end-time revival.

Protection Toolkit

Like all things in the realm of the spirit, there are principles that believers must follow when interacting with it. This is essential because the spiritual realm does not consist solely of the Kingdom of Light—the evil one also roams, seeking whom he may devour (1 Peter 5:8). Understanding and adhering to these principles will help us navigate this realm effectively and safely.

The first principle is to do away with fear and replace it with faith. Fear has no place in the things of the spirit. Let me tell you a story I do not enjoy reminiscing on. In the 1990s, I had a profound encounter with the Holy Spirit when He came with the intention of taking me into the spirit for translation. However, I allowed fear to creep into my heart. That fear made me heavy in the spirit, and I was unable to go. I will always remember this day because it taught me a critical lesson: fear and faith cannot coexist. From that moment, I made the decision to banish fear from my heart and to live by faith alone. In this season, it is vital that we cultivate unwavering faith, for fear will only weigh us down and hinder the move of God in our lives.

The second principle is holiness. Living a holy life is non-negotiable because, as highlighted earlier, the spiritual realm is not only the dwelling place of good spirits but also a battleground where evil spirits operate. Holiness keeps you covered by God, for He is a holy God, and He calls us to be holy as He is holy (1 Peter 1: 15-16). Furthermore, holiness provides a clean conscience, free from the weight of sin, which can become a foothold for the enemy. When we live in holiness, we align ourselves with God's will, ensuring that we are vessels fit for His use and fully protected in the spiritual realm.

The Apostle Paul emphasizes the importance of maintaining a clean conscience alongside unwavering faith:

> *"Keeping your faith [leaning completely on God with absolute trust and confidence in His guidance] and having a good conscience; for some [people] have rejected [their moral compass] and have made a shipwreck of their faith."* 1 Timothy 1:19 (AMP)

This verse underscores how neglecting holiness and a clear conscience can lead to spiritual disaster. Without holiness, our connection to God is weakened, and our faith risks being derailed.

The covering in the blood of Jesus Christ is another vital defensive tool in the realm of the spirit. One time, we were preaching in a small town in Eswatini called Lavumisa. The topic of the sermon was translation, and as we prayed, it became evident that many were going to be translated that very night. This is something we expect to see frequently in this end-time revival, as many translations will occur during moments of prayer.

As we continued in prayer, I felt led by the Spirit to instruct everyone to wash themselves and cover themselves in the blood of Jesus Christ. This is a critical principle in navigating spiritual encounters. As the prayer intensified, some were taken to different places in the spirit. One of the saints was translated to his home area, where he encountered principalities. These spiritual entities tried everything they could to find an opening to accuse him. They even brought up issues related to his relatives and their actions. However, in the realm of the spirit, you cannot be accused for what your relatives have done when you are covered by the blood of Jesus Christ and living a holy life. The blood is a shield, and holiness ensures there are no openings for the enemy to exploit.

This experience underscores the importance of consistent covering in the blood of the Lord Jesus. As we navigate this revival and encounter the supernatural, we must prioritize living a holy life and applying His blood daily to ourselves and our families. Another key layer of protection is staying aligned and right with our spiritual fathers. Their covering serves as an additional safeguard as we engage with the spiritual realm.

Recent Examples

In addition to these remarkable stories, there have been numerous translations since God first spoke to me about them. I recall one particularly compelling testimony shared with me while I was preaching in South Africa. At the end of the service, a man approached me and said, "What you were preaching about has already started happening." I had been teaching about translations and what God revealed concerning them.

He shared how, one time, he thought he was simply dreaming but found himself preaching in China for an entire week. To his surprise, during a conference in South Africa, he encountered a group of Chinese believers who recognized him. They called out his name with familiarity, and, to his astonishment, they told him he had come to preach to them in China. This was undeniable confirmation that he had been supernaturally translated into China to share the Gospel.

This testimony serves as a profound reminder that translations will play a significant role in the spreading of the Gospel during this revival. They will grant access to nations where the Gospel is restricted or outright banned. The world will once again witness that God cannot be limited by human borders or earthly restrictions because the earth belongs to Him.

> *"The earth is the Lord's, and the fullness of it, The world, and those who dwell in it."* Psalm 24:1 (AMP)

Supernatural Evangelism

In fact, God is not limiting the supernatural to unreached or estranged countries; He has also declared that He will move powerfully in the rejected places, even within Christian nations. The Lord has revealed that His supernatural power will extend to bars and brothels across the world. In these unlikely places, God Himself will appear and preach to those who have been written off by society.

I vividly remember an encounter in the 1980s while passing through Matsapha, Eswatini. The Holy Spirit began downloading profound insights into my spirit about these people. God, the master strategist, revealed that once these individuals are saved, they will be easier to use for His purposes than the average Christians. Why? Because, like Paul, they will be wholly sold out to Him, just as they once were to the devil.

These newly saved souls will be radical for God. They will embody a boldness and passion that many believers have become desensitized to over time. For example, they will fearlessly speak in tongues, move freely in the spirit, and operate in the supernatural without concern for human or church protocols. They will carry a raw hunger and willingness to go wherever God sends them, demonstrating His power without hesitation.

This move of God will remind the Church that His Spirit does not operate according to man-made boundaries or societal expectations. These radical converts will redefine what it means to be fully yielded to God, challenging complacency and igniting a fresh fire in the Body of Christ. Their obedience and fervor will reflect the heart of revival: a people wholly consumed by the presence and power of the living God.

Ministration of Angels

God has said that another mark of the manifestation of the supernatural is that He will use angels a lot in this season. The Bible calls angels ministering spirits, which are sent out in service of those who are heirs to salvation. Both you and I are heirs to salvation and angels are meant to come and minister to us.

> *"Are not all the angels ministering spirits sent out [by God] to serve (accompany, protect) those who will inherit salvation? [Of course they are!]"* Hebrews 1:14 (AMP)

Angels will bring messages from God, as they have done throughout biblical history. Just as Peter was freed from prison by the guidance of an angel (Acts 12), we will witness angels helping those in need and delivering divine instructions in this season. Their intervention will become a prominent feature of the supernatural activity during the great end-time revival.

This is not new—angels have been assisting God's people for centuries. We see their activity in the lives of biblical figures such as Abraham, who encountered angels bringing messages from heaven and offering help in critical moments. What's coming now is a heightened manifestation of their involvement.

The Glory

The supernatural removes all physical limitations and takes people to places they do not know. In the 1990s, we were preaching in a place called eBulandzeni, near our first miracle center in Madlangemphisi, Eswatini. We had been invited by another preacher to speak at a tent he was hosting. I arrived on Sunday ahead of the week-long meeting—I was scheduled to start preaching on Monday evening.

While resting ahead of the tent crusade, I heard a voice say something baffling: *"You will not preach in the tent; it will be blown away."* Sunday evening and Monday afternoon services went smoothly. Then, at the end of the Monday afternoon service, a mighty wind blew the tent away, forcing us to quickly relocate to a new venue. We found a small house just in time for my first preaching slot on Monday evening.

As we preached in that service, a prophecy came forth: *"God's glory cloud will come and sweep through this place."* At the time, I spoke the words in obedience and soon forgot them. Later that Friday, having forgotten the prophecy, the Glory cloud descended mightily. People from neighboring villages came without invitation, drawn by the undeniable power of God. Even the next morning, the Glory was still present. In that atmosphere, miracles were happening easily.

I remember young students traveling from a town called Endzingeni, desiring to receive the Holy Spirit. By the time we got to them to pray, we found them already filled with the Spirit because of the Glory cloud. This was just a foretaste of what is coming in this last great revival. There is no limit to what God will do when His Glory manifests.

One remarkable incident involved a woman who fell as she was bringing us food, but, miraculously, the plates she carried did not break and the milk did not spill. While she was on the ground, God took her to heaven. Upon her return, she testified that God had granted her new body parts, including a new heart. Additionally, she was given perfect spiritual vision. These are glimpses of what God is unleashing in this season of the supernatural.

In that same Glory cloud, God began to answer even thoughts. One day, I thought to myself that I desired to preach to dead bodies. At that very moment, as I was preparing to speak, God turned my words into a song in tongues. Many in the congregation came under His power. They were slain in the Spirit, and I found myself unable to speak in my natural language—every word I uttered became a song in tongues. This was a foretaste of what happens in the Glory.

What we experienced during that week was a preview of the supernatural that is about to break out in this final revival. When the Glory descends, nothing remains the same. Translations, glory clouds, and creative miracles will no longer be rare occurrences—they are a part of His divine plan to shake the earth and spread His Gospel. This time, God will send people to places they have never been, bypassing natural limitations like visas, passports, or modes of transport.

Privileged

This is a wonderful day where God has decided to super impose himself on the affairs of man. But we should remain grounded and humble. We are not special, nor were those like Philip or Peter who experienced spiritual translations in the Bible. The key is that this is God's time and season, and He is inviting us to participate in it. It is up to us to prepare ourselves to be part and parcel of what God is doing. Forget any past errors, draw closer to Him, live a Holy life and you will be able to partake.

In the next chapter, we will explore the fire that God is sending to planet Earth—fire that will purify, ignite, and empower His people for this great move of revival.

Chapter Seventeen

I Have Come to Cast Fire

"I have come to cast fire upon the earth, and how I wish that it were already kindled!"
Luke 12:49 (AMPC)

In this revival, God intends to cast His fire upon the earth. This fire is not sourced from human effort, nor even a witch doctor or earthly zeal—it flows directly from the Lord Jesus Himself. As He declared over 2,000 years ago, He did not simply wish for this fire; He came to bring it. Even then, He longed for it to be kindled upon the earth.

The good news for us today is that this fire is meant for the earth, not heaven. Heaven has no need for this fire—it is reserved for revival, transformation, and the fulfillment of God's purposes among humanity. Throughout history, God has set the earth ablaze with His fire, but He has revealed that this coming fire will be unlike anything we have ever seen.

When God spoke to us about this fire, He called it liquid fire—a transformative, consuming fire that will descend upon His people. A closer look at the scriptures shows us that what the Lord Jesus was talking about is beyond the fire of baptism by the Holy Spirit; rather, it is a fire that brings radical transformation to those who encounter it.

Fire that Transforms

In Scripture, fire often symbolizes purification, empowerment, and the presence of God. Yet, the fire that the Lord Jesus speaks of in this passage is unique. It is not just an experience—it is an encounter with the living God that changes everything.

When God revealed this fire to us, He made it clear: when this fire arrives, lives will be transformed. Those bound by old habits and patterns will be completely changed. Many whom we never expected to turn to the Lord will come running to Him, and their growth will be rapid. This fire will not only ignite salvation but will also cause these new converts to grow quickly.

I have often said that what causes people to grow, spiritually, is not the length of time they have been in church, but the quality of what they receive. This fire—this divine encounter with the Lord Jesus Himself—will be the ultimate nourishment, accelerating the maturity of new believers.

Those touched by this fire will grow in the things of God at such a supernatural pace that it will seem as though they have walked with Him for years. The change will be so radical and immediate that many will marvel at the work of God in their lives.

The Fire in Scripture and in Our Time

We see a glimpse of this transformative fire in the Bible when the Lord Jesus met the Samaritan woman at the well. In a single encounter, her life was completely changed. She ran back to her city, boldly proclaiming the Messiah, and led an entire city to the Lord.

- This transformation happened in one afternoon—while the disciples were away buying bread.

- She did not spend years in church before sharing the Gospel.

- Her encounter with Jesus Christ was all she needed.

This is the power of the fire that the Lord Jesus is bringing—a fire that imparts transformation, purpose, and zeal in a moment. Yes, being built and discipled remains important, but this fire will accelerate growth and equip people for their divine assignments.

We are on the verge of the greatest harvest in history. This fire is God's tool to plunder hell and populate heaven.

Similarly, we have already witnessed sparks of this fire in action. I remember an instance in the 1980s while preaching in a tent. A spark of this fire was released, and a woman caught it. When she returned home, she began to do things she did not like doing. She preached to her family and friends, shared the Gospel boldly, and lived out her faith with newfound passion and determination. The fire had transformed her, and her life was never the same.

A Fire That Transforms and Equips

This is what awaits all who encounter this liquid fire. It is not just an emotional experience but an encounter with the living God that leaves no room for complacency or stagnation. This fire will:

- Transform hearts and minds.

- Empower believers for their divine assignments.

- Propel people into their God-given destinies.

- Bring glory to the name of the Lord.

This fire is not only a transformative force for individuals but also a critical element in fulfilling the end-time evangelistic mission. It will recruit and equip laborers for the great harvest, as God raises up Generals for Himself—leaders who will carry this fire into the nations.

These Generals will not only be transformed themselves but will also carry the grace to lift others. When they raise their hands in supplication, God will grant them the ability to pour this liquid fire onto others, igniting a chain reaction of transformation and empowerment.

This liquid fire will bring about a fast transformation in people. We do not know how long it took for John to declare, *"As He is, so are we in this world."* (1 John 4:17), but those who encounter this fire will be transformed in record time.

- This fire accelerates growth in the spirit.

- It bypasses years of struggle and stagnation.

- It propels individuals to their divine purpose almost instantly.

What might have taken decades will happen in moments.

When you mention fire, it often invokes fear in people. But the fire of revival is not coming to destroy—it is coming to purify. This liquid fire is not meant to burn people but to burn away everything that is not holy. It is a refining and forming fire.

When Meshach, Shadrach, and Abednego were thrown into the fiery furnace by King Nebuchadnezzar, the fire did not harm them. Instead, it burned away the ropes that bound them, enabling them to walk freely within the fire (Daniel 3:19-27).

For the end time church, this fire will do the same:

- It will burn away jealousy, pride, and rebellion.

- It will spark love, humility, and the character of God in His people.

Those touched by this fire—people who will perform miracles and be used mightily by God—will still walk in humility. They will submit to one another, following the way of God. This is the fire that the Lord Jesus came to cast upon the earth. And it is coming in this revival.

Fire and Faith

This liquid fire is not just a transformative agent; it is also going to ignite an unshakable faith in those who receive it. You may be reading this and do not feel like you have strong faith. But let me tell you this: those who encounter this fire will walk in faith so strong and immovable that it will equip them to be used mightily in this time. This faith, brought about by the fire, will be the foundation for the unprecedented creative miracles we have spoken about.

As we have said before, this revival will not just be about the ordinary—it will be about the extraordinary. Limbs will grow out, organs will be created, and impossible situations will be reversed. Such creative miracles require a level of faith that goes beyond human understanding, and this liquid fire will bring that kind of faith into the hearts of God's people.

When this liquid fire comes upon you, it won't just refine and transform you; it will infuse you with the faith you need to move mountains. It will position you to be used as a vessel in this great outpouring, enabling you to be a carrier of God's glory and a witness to His unmatched power. This is the kind of faith that the times we are entering demand—a faith that is steadfast, unwavering, and ready to act on the Word of God without hesitation.

The Prophetic Fire Revival

God is raising prophets and prophetic people who will carry this fire. He has proclaimed that the Word in them will be like liquid fire, capable of melting even the hardest of hearts. No heart will be too stubborn or hardened for this fire. This is why this revival will also be called the *Prophetic Fire Revival.* As this revival sweeps across nations, countless lives will be transformed. Even those we once thought unreachable or unsavable will turn to the Lord because of the Word spoken by these prophetic voices. The fire of this Word will consume everything that cannot endure the test and will break even the most stubborn resistance.

Many will come to understand why God's word is like fire. So, when His Word is inside these prophetic people and they speak it, it will be like a fire that will change many hearts.

> *""Is not My word like fire [that consumes all that cannot endure the test]?" says the Lord, "and like a hammer that breaks the [most stubborn] rock [in pieces]?" Jeremiah 23:29 (AMP)*

Oh, how I wish this fire would already be kindled! This is the fire that will transform lives, change hearts, and prepare the Church for the greatest move of God in history. However, as with all things of great value, this fire comes with a price to keep it. The question we will address in the next chapter is this: *Are you willing to pay the price to keep this fire?*

Chapter Eighteen

Are You Willing to Pay the Price?

"Then Jesus said to His disciples, 'Whoever wants to be My disciple must deny themselves and take up their cross and follow Me.'"

Matthew 16:24 (NIV)

Evan Roberts, one of the key figures in the Welsh Revival, often preached sermons filled with profound revelation[1]. During one of his messages, where Roberts was pouring revelation after revelation, a woman in the audience, overwhelmed by the mysteries he was sharing, cried out, "Blessed are the paps (breasts) from which you sucked. I wish I could also know these mysteries." To this, Roberts responded with a sobering question: "Are you willing to pay the price?" There's always a price to pay.

Those who have gone before us paid the price, and it was not easy. It was *not* easy. It was *not* easy. Some were persecuted. Some were thrown into prison. Others faced horrific deaths. Yet, to them, there was nothing more precious than the Kingdom of God. They were willing to endure anything for the sake of His Glory. They counted the cost, and they paid the price.

> **"Others were tortured to death with clubs, refusing to accept release [offered on the terms of denying their faith], so that they might be resurrected to a better life. Others had to suffer the trial of mocking and scourging and even chains and imprisonment. They were stoned to death; they were lured with tempting offers [to renounce their faith]; they were sawn asunder; they were slaughtered by the sword; [while they were alive] they had to go about wrapped in the skins of sheep and goats, utterly destitute, oppressed, cruelly treated."** Hebrews 11:35-37 (AMPC)

As you are reading this, you may have been captivated, fascinated and at times scared at all of the things I have shared with you. But as wonderful and awe-inspiring as the promises of God's revival are, there is a price to pay.

Jesus Christ Paid His Price

In the Garden of Gethsemane, the Lord Jesus Himself paid the ultimate price. The Bible recounts how He was in such deep agony that He sweat drops of blood (Luke 22:44)—grieving not only the physical torment ahead but the weight of the world's sin. You and I may never fully comprehend the magnitude of this price. For a holy God to bear the sins of all humanity—it was an unfathomable cost.

The pain of the nails driven into His hands and feet was excruciating, but that was not the most painful thing for Him. The deepest agony came from being separated from the Father—a separation that occurred for the first time in all of eternity. Why? Because God hates sin, even when it is borne by His only Son.

If it cost Him this much to bring us redemption, we should not be surprised when God asks us to pay a price for His Glory. For sure, He will prepare us for the price we are to pay. When the moment comes, it may feel unbearable.

You may feel like you can't endure it. But I want you to know this: nothing compares to what our Lord endured. His sacrifice serves as both a reminder and an encouragement. If He bore such a price for us, He will strengthen us to bear the price He asks of us.

The Cost of Revival

Beloved reader, as glorious and awe-inspiring as the promises of God's revival are, there is a price to pay.

- For a child, the price may be giving up TV shows, games, or favorite activities—a small thing to an adult, but a great sacrifice for a child.

- For an adult, it may be something much deeper—career ambitions, comfort, personal dreams, or even relationships that hinder complete obedience to God.

- For some, the price is their reputation. People will laugh at them, mock them, and call them fools for pursuing a move of God.

- For others, it will be long hours of prayer—pressing in, contending, and fasting when no one else is watching.

Each of us has a different price to pay. What God asks of you will be tailored to the strongholds or comforts you hold most dear. Some sacrifices will feel unbearable. You may cry bitter tears in secret, wondering if you can endure. But it is in this sacrifice that God refines us, preparing us for His work.

To carry God in this revival, we will have to pay the price of seeking and finding Him. Seeking God is not a casual endeavor—it is a passionate, relentless pursuit, using all the strength within us to chase after Him.

> **"My whole being follows hard after You and clings closely to You; Your right hand upholds me."** Psalm 63:8 (AMP)

When we follow hard after the Lord, it is because we desire nothing but Him. This kind of pursuit refuses to give up until God is found. Our hearts are not chasing blessings, miracles, or signs—they are chasing God Himself. Let me tell you this: it is impossible not to find God when we seek Him with all our hearts.

> **"One thing have I desired of the LORD, that will I seek after; That I may dwell in the house of the LORD all the days of my life, To behold the beauty of the LORD, and to enquire in his temple."** Psalm 27:4 (KJV)

The desire to seek God is not something we can generate on our own. It begins with Him. God, in His infinite love, places within us the hunger to seek after Him. When He reaches out to hold us, it is an unparalleled opportunity to hold Him back—to grab hold of

Him with all we have. When we do, the pursuit transforms into an embrace, and those who witness it will sing in amazement: "Blessed, happy, fortunate is the one who has found the Lord!"

The Generation That Will Find God

This is not a generation like any other. We are the generation called to seek God and find Him. We are the generation destined to see the Lord. Let us rise to the call and pursue Him with unwavering passion, for this is the time to seek and find the One who is the source of it all.

Psalm 63:8 reads, **My whole being, all of me.** This speaks to the depth and intensity with which we are called to seek God—not just with our hearts, but with our hearts, souls, and even our bodies. The psalmist captures this yearning in another place: **"My heart, soul, even my body faints after You." (Psalm 84:2)** This is a complete surrender. A yearning for God that consumes every part of our being. That is where you and I have to reach.

In the time of revival, seeking God is for everyone. It does not matter who you are: young or old, male or female, educated or uneducated. When God plants the desire in your heart to seek Him, nothing can stop you. You will seek Him, and you will find Him. This is the promise for all who hunger after God.

For those who are educated, this can be an advantage—because the more you study creation, the clearer the evidence of God becomes. For example, scientists, in studying galaxies or the fine-tuned design of the universe, often encounter things so wondrous and unexplainable that they are brought to the inescapable conclusion: there is a God. For now, a lot of them are calling it intelligent design, but soon they will come to this clarity.

The pursuit of God leads to the same truth—He is real, He is near, and He desires to be found by those who seek Him with all their hearts.

When we say we are pursuing God, we mean we are seeking after God, not what God can give. It is Him we seek. When you seek money, spouse or employment, it is for yourself. But when you seek the Lord, it is not just for yourself, it is for a generation. You get God for many people. There are many who will find Him because you have found Him.

Tailored Price

The nice thing is that even if I wanted to tell you what your price will be, I couldn't because it will be different from mine. But much like a store, as you draw closer, you will know the price. The cost of following God is uniquely tailored for each one of us. Think of the tailored price that was paid by some of the people who just heard the Lord Jesus say follow me. Peter and Andrew had to leave their boat behind. James and John the family business. Matthew had to walk away from his tax-collecting table. Zacchaeus had to repay everything fourfold. I want you to know, no matter how high the price, it is because He is drawing you closer to Himself. Every challenge, every sacrifice is a step toward greater intimacy with the Savior.

Receiving Jesus Christ is free, but growing in Him comes at a price—a price that God alone determines, and it is often tied to the strongholds in our lives that He wants to break.

- For some, the price may be learning to keep quiet, especially if they are accustomed to talking too much, making it difficult to hear God's voice.

- For others, it may be relinquishing a prized possession, breaking attachments to material things.

- Some will have to learn to prioritize God above every human connection, proving that He is their first love.

Each path is personal, and each price is necessary for our growth and alignment with His will. What He asks of one, He may not ask of another. Your journey is yours alone. Do not compare the cost God asks of you to what He asks of someone else. The amazing thing is, even if you are similar to the next, the price you're required to pay will always be uniquely tailored to you. It's like a custom-made suit—two people may have a similar shape, but a suit tailored for one won't fit the other quite the same. Even the smallest differences in posture or proportion affect the fit.

In the same way, the sacrifices, tests, and stretching God requires of you are specific to your journey. Your cost has been measured according to your calling. So don't look sideways. Don't compare. Just yield—and let Him finish the work in you.

Trust that God knows what lies ahead and that His instructions are for your ultimate good and His glory.

Price of Prayer

Sometimes, the price we pay is prayer—standing in the gap for others.

One day, God dropped a particular family into my spirit while I was praying. This family was dear to me—I had led them to salvation, except for the husband, who was not present at the time.

As I continued praying, the burden for them did not lift. This is a lesson in sensitivity, do not stop praying until the victory comes. Even as I prepared for work, bathed, and went about my day, the urgency remained.

Finally, I called the wife and shared my concerns. She assured me that everything was fine, thanking God with her usual joyful spirit. But that evening, she returned home to find her child trembling with fear.

It turns out a terrifying incident had taken place at the child's school. A man had entered the classroom and threatened to kill everyone if his demands were not met.

Many children escaped, but the man pursued this woman's child, nearly stabbing him. At the last moment, a teacher and a student intervened, saving the child's life. If I had ignored the burden to pray, the outcome could have been terrible.

This is the cost of obedience! Walking with God means acting when He speaks—even if it feels inconvenient or insignificant at the time. Obedience is not about what makes sense to us—it is about aligning with God's perfect will.

Paying in Obedience

Walking with God is not always easy, but it is the only path for those who love Him. **"Obedience is better than sacrifice"** (1 Samuel 15:22). Whether it's learning to keep quiet, giving away something precious, or prioritizing time with Him, the cost is worth it.

God is preparing us for something greater, and our obedience today is shaping the future He has planned for us.

One powerful story of obedience and paying the price is that of the disciples. When the Lord Jesus told them to go and tarry in Jerusalem until the power came, they obeyed. They locked themselves in the Upper Room, waiting for the outpouring of the Holy Spirit.

For ten days, they remained in prayer and unity, not knowing the exact moment when the promise would come. I have often thought about this—perhaps even when they were hungry and someone suggested, "Thomas, why don't you go get some bread?" they refused.

No one wanted to miss what was about to happen.

They were willing to pay the price and wait in expectation—and because of that, the fire came. It changed the world. They paid the price, and that's why it is said of them:

> **"These who have turned the world upside down have come here too."** Acts 17:6 (NKJV)

There were over 500 disciples that Jesus showed Himself to, but only 120 paid the price. Because they paid the price, they carried a fire that shook the earth. Walking with God is never easy, but if you love Him, you will obey.

Are You Willing to Pay the Price?

I have a question; are you ready to pay the price? God may want you to do something that is not popular. God might make you do something that will turn many people against you. You must be willing to pay the price. For some, the price may be hours in prayer. For some, it may be doing something that the Lord demands and will cause them to suffer dire consequences for their decision to obey God. For preachers, it may be standing for the truth. It may be standing and saying, "I won't allow this because it is against the will of God." Everyone will have to pay the price. All the prices are different. It all depends on what it would really cost to break you.

Young people, who God has promised to carry His Glory in this revival, will have to pay the ultimate price—a price that demands their complete surrender, obedience, and pursuit of Him above all else. The mantle that has been promised to this generation is extraordinary, but it requires extraordinary commitment, sacrifice, and dedication.

In the next chapter, we will explore the promise God has made to the young people and the profound role they will play in this end-time revival. We will also share insights from our own journey, offering guidance on the requirements upon them. For them to carry this Glory, they must not only seek Him wholeheartedly but also be willing to pay the ultimate price to live a life set apart for His purposes.

Chapter Nineteen

Young Men of the Provinces

"So Ahab said, "By whom?" And he said, "Thus says the Lord: 'By the young leaders of the provinces.'" Then he said, "Who will set the battle in order?" And he answered, "You.""
1 Kings 20:14 (NKJV)

One of the most exciting revelations God has given us about this revival is that He will use young people in a mightier way than ever before. In fact, God has declared that young people will be at the forefront of this move. Because God has spoken, we know it will surely come to pass.

To every young person, this is a reminder:

- God is not expecting you to fail—He has a plan for your life.

- God is committed to seeing you succeed—He watches over His Word to fulfill it.

- If God has called you, He will equip you.

When it comes to His Word over your life, God Himself is attentive to bring it to pass.

Young People Have Always Been God's Choice

Throughout the Bible, God has consistently chosen young people to accomplish His purposes. Think of Adam in the Garden of Eden—he was only a day old when God entrusted him with the responsibility of naming the animals and everything in the garden. Remarkably, everything Adam named, God agreed with.

Another powerful example is the Lord Jesus Himself. At a young age, He was already teaching scripture in the temple and performing miracles. At just 30 years old, He began the ministry that would forever change the course of history.

This revival will be marked by a similar empowerment of young people. God has chosen them to be His vessels in this time. In 1 Kings 20, Israel was under attack from King Ben-Hadad of Aram. He sent a list of demands to King Ahab, but the final demand was so extreme that Ahab refused.

At that moment, a prophet of God came to Ahab with a message of victory: Thus says the Lord: Have you seen all this great multitude? Behold, I will deliver it into your hand today, and you shall know and realize that I am the Lord.

When King Ahab asked how God would fulfill this promise, the prophet replied, "Thus saith the Lord, Even by the young men of the princes of the provinces."

This is the same prophetic word that God has declared for this end-time revival: young people will be at the forefront, used in mighty ways to ignite and carry the fire of God.

Investing in the Future

Let me tell you this. Any movement without passionate, firebrand young people is doomed to fail. This truth is evident even in secular contexts. When the youth of a nation act in corruption, compromise, or immorality, the future of that nation is in danger. Conversely, when young people rise up and do what is right, there is hope for the future.

Even in the political sphere, the importance of young people is undeniable. One needs to only look at the significance placed on youth league meetings in political parties. These gatherings are often viewed as being crucial as the main party's assemblies because they recognize young people as the bridge between the present and the future. This is the same intelligence the Church must harness as it prepares for the revival.

Churches must deliberately invest in their young people, recognizing them not just as the future of the Church but as its present strength and vitality. Young people are a precious treasure. In our church, we don't see young people as the "future" of Revival Life Ministry; They are Revival Life Ministry. They are integral to what God is doing now. They are not waiting on the sidelines for their time—they are stepping into the field today, and God is equipping them for a mighty harvest.

To every young person reading this: God has called you for such a time as this. You are not an afterthought in His plan for this revival—you are central to it. For the Church at large, this is the time to nurture, equip, and empower young people to take their place as God's chosen vessels for this end-time move.

Separated for Purpose

The word has gone out, but often it comes with a role for us to play. Before God can effectively use young people in this end-time revival, it is crucial that young men and women set themselves straight. God does not want to use young people like donkeys, only to discard them after a short season. He does not desire for them to burn out after ten years of service or to fail along the way. Rather, He desires to use young people consistently and powerfully until the very end of this revival.

When young people carry themselves with integrity, they become standard-setters in the world. They are not merely followers of trends; they are pace-setters, shaping both the Church and the world. Paul encouraged Timothy to live as such a standard, urging him to set the pace for others to follow. This is because the Church should always set the pace for the world.

When Paul chose Timothy as a mentee and co-laborer, he did not rely on a divine vision to select him. Rather, he heard a good report about Timothy's character and conduct. The Word says:

> **"Now Paul traveled to Derbe and also to Lystra. A disciple named Timothy was there, the son of a Jewish woman who was a believer [in Christ], however, his father was a Greek. Timothy was well spoken of by the brothers and sisters who were in Lystra and Iconium."** *Acts 16:1-2 (AMP)*

Timothy's recommendation came not from his age, title, or eloquence but from his lifestyle—a lifestyle that brought a good report. This example highlights an essential principle for young people: your conduct will speak louder than your words. It is very important that, as young people live their lives, they do so in a way that testifies to their commitment to God and His work.

Throughout history, God has always used young people. But what sets them apart is not merely their youth—it is their integrity, obedience, and willingness to be vessels fit for His purpose. In this time of revival, the call is not just to be used by God but to live in such a way that brings glory to His name and sets a godly example for others to follow. Young people must remember: it is not enough to carry the fire—you must also live in a way that honors the God who has entrusted it to you.

Thus, it is very important, even in this lifetime, that young people prepare themselves to be used by God. This preparation starts with living a holy life, walking in tune with the Holy Spirit, and being of good report. If, as a young person, you have been walking in a different direction, let me assure you—it is not too late to start following the way of the Lord. God has a plan for each and every one of us and a unique role for every young person to play in this end-time revival.

It's true, you might have made mistakes. But let me remind you—your mistakes have not disqualified you before God. He still has a purpose for your life, and His plans for you are good. What will empower us to live holy lives is not the fear of judgment, but the deep realization of how much He loves us. When you think about His love, ask yourself: "How can I disappoint the one who loves me so much?"

The thought of His unconditional love will draw you closer to Him and make you drop every sin. Holiness becomes not a burden but a joyful response to His love.

Wisdom to Live Right

A key to living a life of holiness and righteousness is acquiring wisdom from God. When we look at the life of Samuel, we see an excellent example of a young person walking in both wisdom and integrity. Though Samuel was young, God entrusted him with a very difficult message about his mentor, Eli—a task that required both maturity and courage. Samuel shared the message faithfully and respectfully, showing wisdom beyond his years.

Samuel was not just known for the accuracy of his prophecies; he was also known for living an upright life. In this, we see a contrast to Solomon, who is famous for asking God for wisdom. While Solomon's request for wisdom was admirable, he specifically asked for wisdom to govern a nation—not necessarily wisdom to live a life of integrity. Samuel, on the other hand, lived as an example of someone who embodied both.

As we seek God, we should take note of Samuel's life and learn to ask for the kind of wisdom that helps us live a life that brings glory to God. The Bible encourages us to ask for wisdom, and when we do, we should desire wisdom not just for success or leadership, but for the strength to live righteously, to reflect God's love, and to walk in His ways daily.

> **"If any of you lacks wisdom [to guide him through a decision or circumstance], he is to ask of [our benevolent] God, who gives to everyone generously and without rebuke or blame, and it will be given to him."** James 1:5 (AMP)

Just because you are young does not mean that you have to be immature and foolish. One of our brethren once saw a dream from God in which all the young people in the ministry had grey hair. We came to understand this vision to mean that God is going to grant wisdom to young people in an extraordinary way.

The Word of God

While this is the time for young people to be mightily used by God to do tremendous things for His glory, we must also recognize that certain things can disqualify us. For instance, if you do not read the Word, God cannot use you. It's not enough to be on fire for God without being deeply rooted in His Word.

We have mentioned Evan Roberts before and the role he played in the Welsh Revival. One thing that has always fascinated me about his story is his deep devotion to the Word of God. He had a small pocket-sized bible that he took everywhere he went. Even while working in the coal mines with his father, whenever he had a break, he would read it. Evan Roberts' unwavering commitment to scripture prepared him for the mighty role he played in revival. This is the kind of dedication God is calling young people to today. If you want God to use you in this revival, start by making the Bible your closest companion. Read it, study it, meditate on it, and most importantly, obey it.

The psalmist makes it clear that the Word of God has the power to cleanse and purify a young man's heart, preparing him to walk according to God's will:

"How can a young man keep his way pure? By keeping watch [on himself] according to Your word [conforming his life to Your precepts]." Psalm 119:9 (AMP)

God will use young people who treasure the Word in their hearts, and it is that Word that will keep them walking on the right path. In His famous prayer for the Church, the Lord Jesus declared that the Word would sanctify and purify His people. I believe this is particularly relevant for this season, where our young people will need to be purified by the Word to see the promises of God fulfilled in their lives. The days when God used people who did not live right are over.

The Word of God will not only cleanse us but also keep us from going astray. His Word in our life is final. It will check our motives, our decisions, and our actions. One of the recurring issues we see is people praying about things God has already spoken about in His Word. I repeat, do not pray about something God has already ruled on. This is dangerous because it opens the door for deception by the enemy. For example, what use is it to pray and ask, "God, should I go to church today?" when God has already made it clear in His Word that fellowship is vital for our growth:

> **"not forsaking our meeting together [as believers for worship and instruction], as is the habit of some, but encouraging one another; and all the more [faithfully] as you see the day [of Christ's return] approaching."** Hebrews 10:25 (AMP)

Young people must be careful not to go beyond the guidelines of the Word of God. The Word of God is the standard. It doesn't matter how powerful a vision or dream might seem—everything must be checked against the Word. This principle will help us to stay grounded and finish strong.

Living a Submitted Life

In addition to living a life rooted in the Word and walking in holiness, submission is another crucial qualifier for young people during this revival. While God has clearly stated that young people will be at the forefront of this mighty move, they will not move without direction. Instead, they will be guided by their elders, who will direct them on where to go and how to proceed. The picture God gave us is that of arrows in the hand of a warrior—ready and equipped to be launched by their elders.

> *"As arrows are in the hand of a warrior, so are the children of one's youth."* Psalm 127:4 (AMPC)

Submission to the wisdom and authority of elders is essential, and it will play a pivotal role in leading us to victory during this end-time revival. When Joel prophesied about the last army, he described it as one that marches in unity, one that does not break its ranks:

> *"They march each one [straight ahead] on his ways, and they do not break their ranks."* Joel 2:7 (AMPC)

This revival is not just about individual strength or efforts; it is about collective unity under divine leadership. God has promised that He will lead this army, and the older generation will provide the wisdom necessary for the young to fulfill their calling. The strength of the young and the wisdom of the old must work hand in hand. The young will move with vigor and passion, but the elders will provide direction and discernment to ensure their efforts are fruitful and aligned with God's plan.

In these last days, there is no room for division between generations. We need everyone—both young and old—working together in harmony. The wisdom of the older generation is not something that can be bought or replaced; it must be acquired and cherished. To win this spiritual battle, we need unity across generations, with none left behind. Moses demonstrated this principle when he boldly declared that every Israelite, young and old, would be part of the journey to serve the Lord:

> *"Moses said, 'We will go with our young and our old, with our sons and our daughters, with our*

> *flocks and our herds [all of us and all that we have],
> for we must hold a feast to the Lord.'"* Exodus 10:9
> (AMP)

This revival will only reach its full potential when both the young and the old walk side by side. The energy and passion of the youth, combined with the wisdom and experience of the elders, will ensure that God's army remains steadfast, united, and victorious.

Together, we will see the fulfillment of God's promises and witness the greatest revival the world has ever known. But the burden is not on one group alone to make it work. Both the young and the old have roles to play, and each must understand their responsibility in the time we are in. The older generation must embrace the demands of this season and not let jealousy creep in as young people are used mightily by God. At the same time, young people must recognize the value of the wisdom that comes from experience.

Wisdom of the Old

One of the most terrible mistakes a young person can make is to depend solely on the inexperience of their peers instead of leaning on the wisdom of the elderly.

We see a cautionary tale in the life of King Rehoboam. When he ascended to the throne after his father Solomon, he faced a request from his people to lighten their burdens. Initially, he sought counsel from the elders who had advised his father. Their wisdom was clear and sound:

> **"King Rehoboam consulted with the elders who had served and advised his father Solomon while he was still alive and said, 'How do you advise me**

> **to answer this people?' They spoke to him, saying, 'If you will be a servant to this people today, and will serve them and grant their request, and speak good words to them, then they will be your servants forever.'"** *1 Kings 12:6-7 (AMP)*

But Rehoboam ignored this wise advice and instead turned to the counsel of his peers, who urged him to impose even harsher conditions on the people. Their reckless advice led to disastrous consequences:

> **"But he ignored the advice which the elders gave him and consulted the young men who grew up with him and served him."** 1 Kings 12:8 (AMP)

The result? The tribes of Israel rebelled, leaving Rehoboam with only the tribes of Judah and Benjamin. His kingdom was divided, and his reign was marked by failure. This story serves as a powerful warning: there is wisdom in submitting to the leadership and experience of those who have walked ahead of you.

Submission is not just about honoring the past; it is also a safeguard against pride. As God uses young people in this revival to accomplish extraordinary exploits, submission will act as an anchor to keep them grounded. Pride is dangerous, and its consequences are devastating. Lucifer's fall was not because of theft, deceit, or murder—it was because of pride. Pride was the beginning of his downfall, and it can be the downfall of any young person whom God uses mightily if they fail to remain humble.

We have seen throughout history how pride has derailed many who started well in the things of God. Some became so consumed by their pride that God, in His mercy, had to take them home early to prevent them from going astray. It's not that these people wouldn't have reached heaven, but they lost the opportunity to fulfill their full potential and run their race to the very end.

This is why humility and submission are non-negotiable. The fact that God is using young people in this revival is not new—God has used others before, and He will use others after. But those who remain humble and submissive will not only sustain the fire but also carry it further than they ever imagined.

Young people, remember: the race is not about how you start but how you finish. God can rewrite your story. But submission, humility, and reliance on God will ensure that you don't just burn brightly for a moment but shine for a lifetime, fulfilling all that God has spoken over this generation.

It Has Started

There is so much in store for young people in this revival, and we have been blessed to witness early signs of what is coming. Let me share just two powerful stories to spark your curiosity and stir your faith.

A young girl in secondary school had a vision of a man about to hang himself. God commanded her to pray for this man. Imagine, as a young person, having the life of someone in your hands! She obeyed and went into prayer. Later, during a walk, she saw this man carrying a rope. She immediately turned to pray again. She prayed until, in the spirit, she saw the man walk back alive, still holding the rope. Her obedience saved his life.

More recently, during our Prophetic and Apostolic School for the Nations gathering, one of the young people in our church had a vision of people receiving body parts from heaven—hearts, lungs, you name it. In His faithfulness, God moved mightily, and many people were healed.

Young people, this is going to be a time of great exploits! The heavens are calling you—young people, arise! It is your time! It is your season! But to step into this time, you must prepare yourselves. Take your positions and decide, as Daniel did, "I will not defile myself." Though sin may be cheap and easy, you must make the choice to stand apart.

The enemy may lay temptation before you, just as Potiphar's wife tempted Joseph. Joseph didn't go looking for trouble—it came to him, but he chose God. Likewise, you must make that same decision, not just in your songs, but in your actions before the world. It's not enough to sing, "I choose you again and again"; you must actually choose Him again and again, day after day, no matter the cost.

The heavens are watching. The decisions young people make now are being recorded. This is not just a call to a moment of inspiration—it's a call to live a life that says, "I choose God above all else." Young people, the time for the greatest revival on earth is now. Separate yourselves from everything that would hold you back, and choose God with your whole heart.

Chapter Twenty

The Glorious Return

"**B**ehold, He is coming with the clouds, and every eye will see Him, even those who pierced Him; and all the tribes of the earth shall gaze upon Him and beat their breasts and mourn and lament over Him. Even so (must it be). Amen (so be it)."
Revelation 1:7 (AMPC)

One of the greatest revelations God has given us about this revival is that it will never end. Instead, it will continue to grow, moving from glory to glory and wave to wave, until it ultimately ushers to the return of our Lord Jesus Christ. This truth makes it essential for us to prepare our hearts and remain ready, for the exact day and hour of His coming are unknown.

The knowledge of the glory of the Lord will cover the earth just as the waters cover the sea, and no place will be untouched by His mighty move (Habakkuk 2:14). The knowledge of His glory will fill the world in ways far beyond what we can comprehend.

The trumpet shall sound, and in a moment, in the twinkling of an eye, we will be caught up to meet Him. Though some preach against the rapture, human arguments cannot change the plan of God. When the appointed time comes, regardless of debates or doubts, God will take His people. His Word is unchanging and His promises are sure.

And when the Church is caught up, it will not be an escape but a victorious ascent. We will go up in style, as a triumphant Church, a glorious Church, without spot or wrinkle. It will be the ultimate demonstration of God's victory over the powers of darkness. The Church will rise as the redeemed Bride of Christ, radiant and prepared, marking the greatest moment of triumph that heaven has ever displayed.

Some even go as far as to argue that the Lord Jesus has already come back. Many false religions make this claim, but the Bible is clear that He will return the same way He left, and all will see Him. When Jesus Christ ascended to heaven, the angels gave a promise about His return:

> **"This [same] Jesus, who has been taken up from you into heaven, will return in just the same way as you have watched Him go into heaven."** Acts 1:11 (AMP)

This verse assures us that His return will be both visible and unmistakable—just as His departure was. His return is certain. The only unknown factor is His timing—which is solely reserved for the the Father:

> **"But of that [exact] day and hour no one knows, not even the angels of heaven, nor the Son [in His humanity], but the Father alone."** Matthew 24:36 (AMP)

Our responsibility is not to speculate about the timing but to stay ready, prepared, and faithful. We must live with the constant expectation of His return, actively pursuing His will and fulfilling His purpose during this last and greatest revival.

I once saw a vision of a tilted mountain with the words *"Jesus is coming soon"* engraved upon it. Beneath this inscription, I saw inscriptions in six other languages that I did not know, yet in my spirit, I knew they all said the same thing: *"Jesus is coming soon."* In another vision, the Lord showed me six months of intense divine happenings unfolding across the world, culminating in the sound of the trumpet and the rapture of His Church. These visions serve as a powerful reminder that even as we press forward in this great revival, we must keep our eyes on the ultimate hope: the return of our Lord Jesus Christ. His return is closer than ever, but something is even nearer—the explosion of this last and greatest revival.

The first drops of this revival have already begun falling across the world. Imagine clothes hanging on a line during the first drops of rain; you can still run out and bring them inside. But as the rain intensifies, there comes a point where it's impossible to retrieve the clothes. *Seliyana*. It is raining right now. But when the full explosion of this revival hits, nothing will stop this rain of God's Glory.

As you read these words, do not see this revival as for others. I want you to know this: you were chosen for this time. God could have placed you in any generation—in the days of Abraham, Elijah, or even when the Lord Jesus walked the earth—but He appointed you specifically for this moment. You have a specific role in this revival. Consider all the times the devil tried to take your life and failed. In my own life, I was rescued from drowning by a man I had never met. That was not a coincidence. God's hand has been upon you and me - preserving us for such a time as this.

Whilst this is an exciting revelation, it carries a great responsibility. The onus is on us to take our position. God appointed you for this end-time revival without seeking your permission. You are here by His divine appointment and design. Now the choice is yours to fully step into your calling. There is no alternative but to embrace your role, pay the price, die to self, and be ready to carry God's presence to the nations.

I will leave you with this: the heavens are standing on tenterhooks, holding their breath, waiting to see how we will respond to this momentous time, just as they did when the Lord Jesus made His way to the Cross. The last and greatest revival is upon us.

This is your moment! God has chosen you, preserved you, and is calling you to rise. Will you answer the call? Will you prepare yourself and be ready? Let us press forward with our hearts fully surrendered so that when the Lord comes, He will find us faithful and ready to meet Him. The rain is falling; let us run with the fire.

Salvation Decision

"That if you confess with your mouth Jesus as Lord, and believe in your heart that God raised Him from the dead, you will be saved."
Romans 10:9 (NASB)

If you desire to be part of this great revival, salvation is the first step. Salvation is not just an invitation to revival; it is the doorway to eternal life with Jesus Christ. The Bible makes it clear in the verse above.

Salvation is not about what you can do for God; it is about receiving the gift He has already given through His Son, Jesus Christ. It is an act of faith and surrender. By acknowledging your need for a Savior, turning away from sin, and believing in His death and resurrection, you enter into a new life.

If you are ready to take this step and invite Jesus Christ into your heart, pray this prayer with sincerity:

"Heavenly Father, I come before You, acknowledging that I am a sinner in need of Your grace. I believe that Jesus Christ is Your Son, that He died on the cross for my sins, and that You raised Him from the dead. Today, I confess Jesus as my Lord and

Savior. I turn away from my sins, and I surrender my life to You. Lord, fill me with Your Holy Spirit, guide me in Your truth, and help me live in obedience to Your will. Thank You for saving me, for forgiving me, and for giving me eternal life. In Jesus' name, I pray, Amen."

If you prayed this prayer with faith, you are now a child of God! Heaven is rejoicing over your decision. Welcome to the family of God and the beginning of a new life in Christ.

As you begin this journey, I encourage you to:

- Read the Bible daily to grow in your knowledge of God's Word.

- Pray continually to build a personal relationship with Him.

- Connect with a local church where you can grow in fellowship with other believers.

This revival is not for the saved alone—it is for those who hunger and thirst for God. And now, you are part of the army God is raising for this great move. You are ready to carry His presence, His Word, and His power to the ends of the earth.

If you have prayed this prayer, please continue on to the Connect with Us page after the bio. We would love to hear from you.

About the author

Apostle Dr. Mandlenkhosi Simelane is a seasoned servant of God, visionary leader, and devoted family man with over four decades of ministry. He has dedicated his life to advancing God's Kingdom and preparing the Church for the greatest revival in history. Known for his prophetic insight and powerful teachings, Apostle Simelane has traveled extensively, witnessing countless lives transformed through miracles, signs, and wonders.

Apostle Simelane is the founder of Revival Life Ministry, conceived in 1989 and established in 1992. God spoke to him audibly on three occasions, saying, "Go demonstrate My power and make My voice heard." This vision gave birth to the ministry, symbolized by three colors: rich grass green for revival, yellow for life, and white for ministry. Through his ministry, Apostle Simelane has witnessed God's mighty hand move across Africa, Asia, Europe, and beyond, paving the way for the global revival God revealed to him. He has also been called to minister in remote villages, bringing the Gospel to forgotten places and igniting revival in the most unlikely places.

Apostle Simelane is also a loving father and grandfather, whose heart extends beyond his immediate family to many others. Together with his late wife, he has been blessed with many children—seven biological, two by marriage, and several adopted—and has three grandchildren. His love for his family reflects his passion for community and the Church, as he believes that strong families are essential for carrying God's Glory in this end-time revival.

Apostle Dr. Mandlenkhosi Simelane has dedicated over 40 years to ministry, proclaiming and equipping believers for revival. God gave him a vision to raise a generation for revival, and he faithfully serves as the principal of the Prophetic and Apostolic School for the Nations, where believers are prepared for the global move of God. He also provides spiritual oversight to several apostolic ministries and oversees the Global Apostolic Network, a platform dedicated to equipping individuals for revival. In recognition of his immense contribution to the preaching of the Gospel, Apostle Dr. Simelane was honored with a Doctorate from the Breakthrough International Bible University, USA. Through his unwavering dedication and tireless efforts, he has impacted countless lives, spreading the message of Christ with power and conviction.

Through this book, Apostle Simelane shares the wisdom and revelations God has entrusted to him, offering practical guidance and spiritual encouragement for the move of God that is already unfolding. Whether preaching, teaching, or writing, his mission remains the same: to equip believers for their role in the final and greatest revival before the return of Jesus Christ.

Connect with us

Thank you for reading *The Last and Greatest Revival*! We believe that this message is part of God's divine plan for the final move, and we would love to stay connected with you. Particularly new converts, so that we help you on this new journey.

1. Follow Us Online
Stay updated on teachings, prophetic insights, and revival updates:
- **Facebook**: @ApostleDrMandlenkhosisimelane

- **Facebook**: https://www.facebook.com/revivallifeministry

- **YouTube**: @mbabanemiraclecentre8779

- **Youtube**: @ApostleDrMandlenkhosisimelane

2. Visit Our Website
Explore more about our ministry, access additional resources, and stay informed about upcoming events. Visit us at: www.revivallifeministry.org

3. Contact Us

For prayer requests, testimonies, or inquiries, reach out to us at:
- **Email**: ApostleMASimelane@RevivalLifeMinistry.org

May the fire of revival continue to burn in your life!

4. Scan the QR Code

You can reach us by scanning the QR Code below.

May the fire of revival continue to burn in your life!

Endnotes

Introduction: Seliyana

1. The Evening Express and the Evening Mail. "Revival Edition." The Evening Express and the Evening Mail, 16 Jan. 1905, p 1

2. "Twenty Thousand Converts in South Wales." *The Guardian* [London, Greater London, England], 31 Dec. 1904, p. 8.

3. "Weird Babel of Tongues." *Los Angeles Daily Times*, 18 Apr. 1906, p. 1.

Prayer is the Engine for Revival

1. *"John Hyde, Missionary to India – An Apostle of Prayer (Part 3)." Herald of His Coming*, Aug. 2014, http://www.heraldofhiscoming.org/index.php/107-past-issues/2014/aug14/1132-john-hyde-missionary-to-india-an-apostle-of-prayer-part-3-8-1. Accessed 9 Mar. 2025.

Are You Willing to Pay the Price?

1. "1904 Welsh Revival." Baptist Churches Wales, www.bcwales.org/1904-welsh-revival. Accessed 9 Mar. 2025.

www.ingramcontent.com/pod-product-compliance
Lightning Source LLC
Chambersburg PA
CBHW051432290426
44109CB00016B/1519